The Making of Ministry

The Making of Ministry

Edited by

Angela Shier-Jones

✛ EPWORTH

British Library Cataloguing in Publication data

A catalogue record for this book is available
from the British Library

978 0 7162 0644 6

First published in 2008
by Epworth
4 John Wesley Road
Werrington
Peterborough PE4 6ZP

Typeset by Regent Typesetting, London
Printed and bound in the UK by
MPG Books Ltd, Bodmin, Cornwall

Contents

Contributors

Sheryl Anderson is a Methodist minister serving as the Director of the South London Mission, a Methodist social outreach project in London. Her background is in teaching and social work in both the statutory and voluntary sectors. She has served as mentor and tutor for several student ministers as well as chair of the Oversight Committee for Methodist Ministerial Students of the South East Institute for Theological Education.

Justine Allain Chapman is Vice-Principal and Director of Practical Theology at the South East Institute for Theological Education. She is an Anglican priest who has worked as a curate and vicar in south London. She lives in Rochester with her husband and four children where she is attached to the cathedral when not working with ordinands.

Angela Shier-Jones is the Director of Academic Studies and Research at Wesley College, Bristol. She is a Methodist minister who has been involved in theological education for over 15 years. As well as writing and teaching theology, she serves as an educational consultant for VLE (Virtual Learning Environment) curriculum design and delivery for theological education and ministerial formation in both the UK and Europe.

Mark Wakelin is Secretary Designate for Internal Relationships for the Methodist Church. He is a Methodist minister with a particular interest in spirituality and education. He has been a circuit minister, prison chaplain, hospice chaplain, National Secretary of the Methodist Association of Youth Clubs and Director of the Guy Chester Centre. He was editor of the College of Preachers' *Journal* and remains a tutor for the college.

Roger Wiig is the Superintendent Minister of the Bromley Methodist Circuit in London. He taught group dynamics at a postgraduate level in Melbourne, Australia, participated in the training of supervisors for the Uniting Church's Theological College in Brisbane, Australia and co-leads the 'Stronger Together' course (building the skills of reflective praxis) for ministers at the Guy Chester Centre in London.

Kenneth Wilson is a Methodist minister whose ministry has been largely concerned with education. He has served as lecturer in philosophy and ethics at Wesley College, Bristol; Principal of Westminster College, Oxford; and Director of Research at the Queen's Foundation, Birmingham. He is currently a Visiting Research Fellow at Chichester and Canterbury Christ Church Universities, Deputy Director of a Research Programme on character education, and a member of 'Ecclesiological Investigations', an international research programme focused on the theology of the Church.

Jeremy Worthen is the Principal of the South East Institute for Theological Education, which prepares men and women for ordained ministries within the Anglican, Methodist and Lutheran Churches through programmes of part-time study. He has worked in theological education and ministerial formation for over ten years.

Introduction

But you are a chosen race, a royal priesthood, a holy nation, God's own
people, in order that you may proclaim the mighty acts of him who
called you out of darkness into his marvellous light. (1 Peter 2.9)

The ordained ministry in the United Kingdom has had a chequered history
over the last two centuries. It has been loved and feared, despised and
caricatured by politicians, artists and authors alike. Yet throughout it all,
it has managed to retain a dignity and integrity of purpose that has
ensured the continuity of respect for the Church and reverence for God,
until now. The last two decades have seen the ministry brought into
serious disrepute. There has been a significant number of high-profile
prosecutions against ordained ministers for child sex abuse. Some ministers, including some bishops, have publicly questioned the traditional
doctrines of the Church. Groups of gay Christians have disrupted synods
and 'outed' gay clergy. Gay bishops have been vilified by other Christians
on television, on the radio and in the evangelical press. Meanwhile, 50 per
cent of the Catholic population are still denied the opportunity to test
their vocation to ordained ministry in spite of living in a time when
national legislation prohibits discrimination on the grounds of sex in
almost every other sphere of life.

All of this prompts several related questions. Are these things indicative
of some sort of failure in the making of ministry, or are they part of a wider
cultural and sociological problem over which the Church has little or no
control? How can a calling to ordained ministry be discerned and understood in an age when the individual is all important and the cult of the
celebrity dominates what it means to be successful in life? What part can
theological education play in making a ministry that is not only effective in
providing pastoral care to existing congregations, but in challenging and
changing the Church so that it is better equipped to reach out and evan-
gelize in what is considered to be the post-Christian age? Is there any real
value in the difference between ordained and lay ministry to a society that
demands equality of opportunity and insists on living in a meritocracy?
What skills do modern ministers need in order to practise their ministry,

and how should they be acquired? Is there any way of making ministry more accountable, and if so, to whom? And finally, what sort of ministry do church members actually want?

The purpose of this book is to participate in the sort of discussions that it is hoped might eventually lead to productive answers to some of the above questions. All of the contributors are involved in some way in the making of ministry, and have learned to value the wider conversations that a book such as this can provoke. Issues of power and authority, management, accountability and professional capabilities must be brought into dialogue with grace, Scripture, mission and theology for the sake of the future ministry of the Church.

In spite of increasing secularization, there has never been a greater interest in religion and concern for spiritual well-being, and this has led to an increasing demand for chaplains willing to minister in the armed forces, hospitals, prisons, universities, businesses and schools. Cathedral and city mission congregations have been steadily rising over the last ten years. More and more local churches and circuits are engaged in some form of evangelistic enterprise, which they report as beginning to bear fruit. Circuits and districts, parishes and dioceses are reshaping themselves for mission, all of which will require appropriate forms of ministry. The contributors to this book are all involved to a greater or lesser degree by their roles in theological education and their oversight in the process that determines what is or is not an appropriate form of ministry and how it is made.

This book is primarily concerned with ordained ministries, not because lay ministry is deemed in any way less worthy of attention, but so that attention might be drawn to the blurring of boundaries between different forms of ministry that has taken place over the last few decades. Nonetheless, much of what is written about ordained ministry in this book can be directly applied to lay ministry. More importantly, the chapters draw attention to the fact that the distinction between ordained and lay ministries is not one of value, as both are essential for the Church to fulfil its divine calling.

The book falls naturally into two halves, each containing four chapters. The first half explores the theological and practical questions surrounding vocational discernment, training and formation up to and including ordination. The second half reflects on the continuing formation of ministry that results from engagement with the privileges, joys, difficulties and realities of contemporary ordained ministry. In particular, it examines how and why important issues and contexts, often imported from the secular world, have a role to play in shaping and developing ministers and their ministry long after ordination.

Part 1 begins with Chapter 1, 'Calling and Vocation', exploring vocational discernment. It argues that the way in which Churches encourage and enable vocational discernment is a theological statement concerning the divine participation of God in the life of the Church. All Christians share a common vocation to grow in grace and holiness, and individual vocations are valid only inasmuch as they are an integral part of the priesthood of all believers. It is God who calls people to ministry, but the task of discerning the form that that ministry can take within the royal priesthood inevitably falls to the Church.

The assumption that fitness for ministry will be evidenced by specific gifts and abilities forms the basis for most historical and contemporary ministerial discernment in spite of significant scriptural and experiential examples of God calling people who believed they were decidedly ill equipped to fulfil their God-given vocation. The question of what the necessary prerequisites are for specific ordained vocations is a source of considerable division and debate within the Church. All denominations have developed their own criteria based on their understanding of the work and theology of ministry as an office of the Church. Each Church attempts to hold the balance between a belief that God can and does equip those who are called to ministry and the need to ensure that those who are called do not endanger the divine purpose of the Church by being in some way unable to fulfil their ordained responsibilities. What they seek therefore is some evidence or indication that the candidate is not only called to ministry, but is called specifically to ministry within the Church – all of which presumes that the Church knows the forms of ministry that it needs and that God desires it to have. The development of the selection criteria for those offering for pioneer ministers is a case in point but one which also highlights the fact that something more than fitness for ministry lies behind an authentic call to ordained ministry.

The degree to which the social, political, economic and missiological context predetermines those whom the Church is willing and able to authenticate as having a calling to the ordained ministry is important to the debates surrounding the ordination of homosexuals, of women to the episcopate, and of pioneer ministers to fresh expressions of Church. It is examined in Chapter 1 by reflecting theologically on three very different but highly significant variations in the societal and ecclesial perceptions of ministry. First, the general perception of ministers serving in the Church of England was radically altered following the significant changes to ministerial criteria and theological education in the 1900s. Second, a significant mismatch has developed in Africa between the perception of ministry as a profession and the economic reality of the role. Third, the

British Government has recently begun to foster a perception of Islamic ministry as dangerous and needing to be more tightly controlled following the rise of religious fundamentalism. These three illustrations combine to highlight the complexity of the task confronting the Church as it tries to balance discerning the call of God in those who seek to minister to the world with the practical realities dictating the cultural context of contemporary ministry.

The fact that calling is shaped and defined at least in part by the context of ministry does not negate it, however. Every authentic call to ministry, lay or ordained, can be tested against three common characteristics: the longing to minister, the sense of inadequacy for the task, and the compulsion to pursue the calling wherever it might lead. Those called to the ordained ministry will also evidence the characteristic compulsion to embody the truth, and in so doing, play a leading and directing role in the spiritual formation of others as well as themselves.

Chapter 2, 'A Model of Ministerial Formation', picks up on the Victorian model of theological education mentioned in the first chapter and critiques its contribution to contemporary ministerial formation. It begins by exploring the concept of ministerial formation as a specific instance of professional formation which must be coupled with appropriate spiritual formation. The ordained vocation is a professional vocation that is inescapably determinative of the spiritual formation of all those who are called to it. At the same time, it is also a spiritual vocation with professional responsibilities, necessitating professional formation. Ministerial training must therefore address both the spiritual and professional formation of the individual to be effective. The theological basis for this approach to ministerial training is explicated with reference to Scripture and Augustine's outline of the journey of spiritual formation as a restoration of the divine image in the human mind.

The distinctiveness of ministerial formation is ultimately derived from the ministerial vocation which, it is argued, is a gift of God to the Church and the world. Because it is a gift, it shares in the mystery of freedom, divine and human. Accordingly, ministry cannot be said to follow automatically from the acquisition of certain skills or attributes, or even from the need of the Church for people to fill various offices or perform specific tasks. It is God given, for life. In a way that is analogous with marriage, ordination is lifelong and character changing, with permanent responsibility to the 'other' with whom vows have been exchanged and promises have been made. It is thereby linked inextricably to the spiritual vocation of all baptized Christians.

The language of 'being, knowing and doing' can be correlated with

Augustine's mental trinity of 'remembering, knowing and willing' to illustrate the challenges and opportunities presented when ministerial education wrestles with the interrelated dimensions of spiritual and professional formation for ordination. This highlights the need for a continual dialogue between the professional and the spiritual trajectories of ministerial formation. The Victorian model of full-time residential seminaries must therefore be critiqued according to its ability to create and sustain a Christian community in which that dialogue can take place effectively. The chapter concludes with a description of the sort of community that can foster such dialogue and illustrates how this could fit in to both the part-time and full-time residential models of ministerial training currently provided by the Church. In so doing, it challenges the 'contract' model of theological education based on the expectation of certain learning outcomes or professional competencies and argues that spiritual formation is the work of the 'free spirit of the sovereign God'. Sustaining the sort of communities necessary for effective and appropriate ministerial education to take place will be costly both in terms of time and money. Formation is not something that can be hurried. It should, however, be invested in through the appropriate formation of distinctive communities of formation. That knowledge is perhaps the most important thing bequeathed by the Victorians to this generation with regard to ministerial education.

The distinctive communities that are formed today, whether in colleges or on part-time courses, are radically different from those envisaged in the Victorian era. For the first time in the history of the Church, training institutions are achieving something of a balance in their student numbers with regard to gender. This balance is, however, totally at odds with the current balance of power in the Church. While students in training are being prepared to minister in the 'Church of tomorrow', they still need to function in the 'Church of today'. Chapter 3, 'Gender, Spirituality and Power in Ministerial Formation', begins the necessary process of understanding the impact of this change in gender balance on the future Church, and on those currently training for some form of ordained ministry.

The chapter starts with an overview of the current situation with regard to women's leadership in the Church and suggests that there are two areas emerging from earlier research that can offer important insights into the ministerial and spiritual formation of women preparing for ministry. The first is the differences in the faith development and spirituality of women as opposed to men. The second is the experiences and behaviour of women in male-dominated industries.

Women's faith development is a relatively new area of research but one which has profound implications for ministerial training given that spiritual development must be held in balance with professional development. Slee's doctoral research is drawn on extensively to explicate the implications for ministerial training of each of the three generative themes which she identified as revealing women's faith development, namely alienation, awakenings and relationality.

Her theme of alienation is recognized first as being the most difficult to address in ministerial formation where there is a tacit understanding that ordained ministers need to speak of faith in a manner that is confident and certain. This actively inhibits the expression of the necessary doubts and questioning that ministerial formation provokes as part of the spiritual development of the ordinand.

Second, the educational and pastoral practices of the institutional Church are identified as being largely unable to engage with the necessary methodologies to allow women's experiences to 'awaken' them to their spirituality. In spite of the fact that a significant proportion of school and higher educational teaching is now deliberately experientially based and contextually framed in order to relate theoretical with abstracted learning, there is little evidence of this pedagogy being carried through into theological education.

Lastly, the common Christian emphases of self-giving, self-emptying, surrender and of submission can be highly detrimental to the formation of a woman's self-esteem and hence her ability to form confident, equal, spiritual and ecclesial relationships. Many women recognize the language, if not the theological concept, from their direct experience in the home and as lay members of the Church, and hence have difficulty in relating these emphases as part of the necessary formation of strong leadership, power and governance in the Church.

The shift from being a lay woman to being ordained is not dissimilar to the professional change when a woman moves from being a member of staff to a position on the board in business. Lessons from research into this area could therefore be brought to bear on the problem within the Church of so few women being willing to accept positions of responsibility due to their internal doubts, fears and misgivings which are the direct consequence of an abiding lack of self-confidence. This would entail the provision of training which deliberately fosters a genuine belief in the individual and in her ability to wield the power and authority vested in the office which she will hold by affirming the diversity of gender as a positive contribution to the needs of the Church.

The power and authority implicit in ministry, even ministry that is described as servant ministry, are directly related to theological education and ministerial formation. Chapter 4, 'Made for Ordination', therefore addresses the relationship between making and ordaining ministers. The practice of making ministry to order is explored first, drawing on the example of changes made to ministerial training in response to the missiological situation of the Church following the First World War. This highlights the risk of one particular focus – whether parish ministry in the 1930s, or fresh expressions in the new millennium – permanently altering the character of ordained ministry. The Church clearly has a formidable task to do in determining criteria which on the one hand safeguard the integrity of ordained ministry, and on the other hand are still sufficiently open to the Spirit of God at work, so that the Church can respond to the missiological needs of the age.

The historical practice of the ordination of infants provides a useful contrast to the idea that ordained ministry is predominantly predetermined by certain expectations. These expectations arise largely out of the specific ecclesial contexts in which ministries are determined; denominational differences do matter. Not all Churches have a threefold order of ministry, some have only one, others two. This diversity suggests that ministry is shaped if not actually made by the Church, albeit for the best theological or sociological reasons.

The diaconate, for example, is a distinct permanent parallel and equal order of ministry within the Methodist Church, whereas although it can be permanent in the Anglican and Catholic traditions, it is more commonly the first order of a threefold sequential order of ministry.[1] The differences with regard to presbyteral ministry are even more significant between the Reformed and the Catholic traditions. The Catholic tradition implies that ministers are not made, but appointed, to speak in the name of Christ himself. This is contradicted, however, by the fact that it is the Church which decides the criteria for determining whether or not someone can be appointed. The Reformed tradition places greater emphasis on the representative role of the minister as someone who is called by God and set apart for this task by the people of God. Both traditions thus seem to imply that ordination only confirms what the Church has already decided with regard to ministry rather than actively creates it.

To argue in favour of ordination as more than a confirmation of the work of the Church necessitates wrestling with the ontological, incarnational and spiritual dimensions of ordination. The ontological dimension cannot be dismissed as an anachronistic metaphysical conundrum. When recognized as a continual process rather than a single act, ordination evidently effects a permanent change in the character, identity and relationality of the person concerned. The incarnational aspect of ordination provides an alternative understanding of the way in which the context of ministry deliberately shapes and makes the minister. In particular, it helps to explain the role of the traditional Church in raising up and nurturing radical and pioneer ministers. It locates the apostolic succession not in the hands of bishops, but in the ministry of all those who have participated in God's work of reconciliation. The incarnational dimension of ministry also determines the threefold representational role of the minister as the one who represents the Church to the world, Christ to the world, and the Church and the world to God as one who loves them and who is prepared to give up everything for them in obedience to Christ. Finally, the spiritual dimension of ordination highlights the dependence of every aspect of ministry on God's grace. Ordained ministers need to cultivate the same spiritual gifts as all Christians in order to grow in grace and holiness. The only unique gift that God gives to the one who is ordained is that of sacramental character, the wherewithal to join with God in making a moment and a people holy.

Ordination, far from being a service of confirmation, can be highly formative of ministry, something which should be taken into consideration in the theological education of ordinands. The role of the Church in identifying and preparing people for ordination can be viewed positively as safeguarding the tradition and the teaching which inspire and motivate people to seek ordination to both the royal priesthood through their baptism, and to holy orders.

The importance of tradition is highlighted in Part 2 of the book, which deals with the formational dimensions of the context and practice of ministry. Chapter 5, 'Professional, Purposeful, Ecclesial and Liturgical', offers a radical view of tradition not in terms of ecclesial structures or even confessional statements but as that which grows out of the natural human search for meaning. The work of the Church can then be recognized as giving attention to God on behalf of all creation and for all humankind. The purpose of the Church, the chapter argues, is to celebrate in worship God's presence in Christ, and, assisted by the Holy Spirit, to attempt to understand and communicate what this means for every aspect of life, whether public or private. Its success will depend on the willingness of its members to support one another so that it can draw on every available discipline of human enquiry.

The role of the minister, which flows from their sacramental identity, is to lead the community of faith to enquire into the nature of the world and the human experience of it as their response to the gift of grace in Christ that they receive. The task is unending, but that should not daunt either the minister or the community. What is important is doing what can be

8

done, drawing on the limitless resource of God's love to achieve it. The everyday pressures of life can often act to undermine this and other central truths of Christian life. Consequently, people need to be reminded by joining with others and rehearsing the story of the faith. The search for meaning is thus grounded and renewed in the celebration of the liturgy.

The extraordinary responsibilities of the minister to preside at the Eucharist, to encourage and inspire the exploration of God's creation and the meaning of God's presence in the world, demands that the minister undergoes appropriate formation. Being formed for ministry entails letting go of certainty and finality and being open to the discovery of what God is still doing in creation. This is often a painful rather than an immediately liberating experience, but it also helps to prepare the minister for the pain that they will encounter when they share in the formation of others. Formation includes the acquisition of knowledge as well as skills. This should not be limited to knowledge of Scripture, liturgy and the tradition of the Church, but should include subjects such as philosophy, science, and of course, theology. Properly understood, formation involves developing the full potential of human nature; it is a lifelong process that is costly but rewarding.

Chapter 6, 'Ministry, Spirituality and Strategy', picks up the continuity of formation by providing practical guidelines for how ministers can develop effective management skills to complement their spiritual and ministerial skills. It argues that there are two major errors generally made by ministers with regard to management: either they ignore management altogether or they assume that management techniques can be directly applied to ministerial contexts without any adaptation or modification. What ministers as professional managers need to do is engage theologically with the best secular approaches to organizational management with a view to improving the organization and management of the Church.

Professional management skills are needed for more than organization in the Church; pastoral relationships also need to be managed, particularly in the light of the complexity of today's pastoral relationships. This entails a commitment to developing a deeper understanding of pastoral responsibilities and ministerial power. Chapter 7, 'Ministerial Accountability and Continuing Vocational Development', explores models developed in Churches around the world which have been designed to help clergy accept professional responsibility for the way in which they exercise their ministry and maintain both the boundaries of the pastoral relationship and the quality of their ministry through reflection and education.

The chapter begins by contrasting the experiences of good ministerial practice in the Churches of the southern hemisphere with the paucity of accountability in those of the northern hemisphere. The lack of a more concerted engagement with these issues in some Churches is attributed to a reluctance to make continued ministerial development a priority, and a lack of clear standards for the practice of ordained ministry.

Appropriate supervision is an essential component of all good pastoral relationships. Ministers are willing to offer supervision, but are often reluctant to accept it for themselves. Ministry cannot be practised in isolation. Every minister is directly accountable to those they minister to, to the Church, and to God. Ministers therefore share a mutual accountability and a responsibility to develop the following qualities and competencies:

* A growing faith and spirituality that will sustain their lives in ministry.
* A conscious and critical commitment to ministry and mission.
* Knowledge and appreciation of the tradition of the Church.
* Skills appropriate for their particular ministry.
* Critical imagination.

Unfortunately, ministerial accountability or supervision is often thought of as representing hierarchical discipline and authority rather than a means of offering mutual support. For this reason, the chapter concludes by providing an illustration of an alternative form of mutual accountability, namely of peer coaching. Not only is this process described in some detail, but an example format for the presentation and responses of a peer coaching group is provided to encourage the establishment of such groups by those who read the chapter.

The final chapter, 'Living with the Consequences', also addresses the issue of ministerial accountability, but from the perspective of the members of a minister's congregation. Its findings are based on the results of a survey conducted in the (then) London South East District of the Methodist Church concerning the nature and quality of the ministry received. The survey was designed to test the hypothesis that it should be possible to ascertain by enquiry the distinct characteristics of ministry which a congregation believed made a minister a 'good' minister.

An institutional attempt ten years ago to define 'good' ministry highlighted several tensions in the role of the minister resulting from them being 'of the people' yet 'not of the people'. The survey set out deliberately to discover what 'good' meant in terms of quality and ability in spite of the fact that 'goodness' is notoriously difficult to quantify. The results of the questionnaire suggest that a congregation is aware of the dilemma but is nonetheless able to articulate what they mean by 'good' both in terms of expected outcomes and internal responses.

The results of the questionnaire suggest that there is a significant overlap between what the institution values in ministry as evidenced by pre- and post-ordination training syllabi and what congregations value. Above all, good ministers are recognized as those who form good attachments. The congregational responses to the questionnaire and the interviews that were conducted appear to suggest not only that good ministers are being made, but that they are made 'good' through their interaction with and relationship to people and to God.

In the end, therefore, the book concludes where it began, in the divine initiative of God to work with all those willing to wrestle with what it means to live with integrity the life of the baptized as a member of the royal priesthood. Theological learning, the acquisition of multiple professional and spiritual skills and the formation of various characteristics play the smallest part of the making of good ministry. The incarnational grace of God in each and every human relationship is the one essential ingredient for the making of ministry in each and every generation.

Notes

1 The orders are cumulative in that once someone is ordained deacon in the Anglican or Catholic tradition, they remain a deacon, even if subsequently ordained priest or bishop.

Part I

Formed for Ministry

Calling and Vocation

ANGELA SHIER-JONES

Now there are varieties of gifts, but the same Spirit; and there are varieties of services, but the same Lord; and there are varieties of activities, but it is the same God who activates all of them in everyone. To each is given the manifestation of the Spirit for the common good. To one is given through the Spirit the utterance of wisdom, and to another the utterance of knowledge according to the same Spirit, to another faith by the same Spirit, to another gifts of healing by the one Spirit, to another the working of miracles, to another prophecy, to another the discernment of spirits, to another various kinds of tongues, to another the interpretation of tongues. All these are activated by one and the same Spirit, who allots to each one individually just as the Spirit chooses.

1 Corinthians 12.4–11

Introduction

In 2006, for the first time, more women than men were ordained as clergy in the Church of England. Of the 478 clergy ordained in 2006, 244 were women and 234 men. This was a significant milestone in the history of the making of ministers in the Church of England, not only because of the change in gender balance, but also because of the change in ministry that accompanied it. Most of the women were ordained to non-stipendiary, or unpaid, posts, such as assistant priests, with only 95 ordained to full-time stipendiary, or paid, ministry. Does this represent a change in the way God is calling men and women to ministry, or an attempt by the Church to shape and change the calling of women for the priesthood into something that may be more ecclesiastically manageable?

The way in which churches encourage and enable vocational discernment is, without doubt, as much a theological as a practical or ecclesiological statement. Regardless of how they are interpreted, figures such as those quoted above make it all too evident that the understanding of who or what a minister is, and what it is that they are called to be, has changed. The circuit minister, the parish priest and the local pastor have changed almost out of recognition in just 50 years. Ordained ministers are not always white, male and middle class, neither are they necessarily called to full-time stipendiary ministry to a local church or circuit. There has been a significant change in those offering for ordained ministry: the age, gender, social standing and educational ability of many ministerial candidates are radically different from what was once considered the 'norm'. All of which prompts the question, 'Who is God calling – and why?' along with the complementary question 'Who is the Church calling – and why?' It would be far too presumptuous (even if it is highly desirable) to simply assume that the two callings are one and the same. So a third question needs to be asked: 'Are these two callings reconcilable in such a way that the work of the kingdom can flourish and grow?'

This chapter explores these questions, and then proffers some tentative answers by making explicit the context, theology and practicalities that often predicate the conscious decisions of both Church and individuals to respond to a calling to ministry and enable them to discern the proper outcome.

Defining vocation

Holiness is the universal vocation of every person. It is the main road onto which converge all the little paths that are particular vocations.

In Verbo Tuo, Final Document of the Congress on Vocations to the Priesthood and to Consecrated Life in Europe, Rome, 1997

All Christian vocation has its origin in God's gracious call for humanity to be 'holy' as recorded in Scripture:

Like obedient children, do not be conformed to the desires that you formerly had in ignorance. Instead, as he who called you is holy, be holy yourselves in all your conduct; for it is written, 'You shall be holy, for I am holy.'

1 Peter 1.14–16

Calling or vocation is a twofold action – a calling out of or away from one way of living, and towards conformity to the purposes of God – to be holy, to be Christlike, to be reconciled. It is perhaps not surprising therefore that the etymological root of the word for Church, '*ecclesia*', refers to a gathering that is 'called out'. The Church is a gathering of all those who have been called out of darkness and into light (1 Peter 2.9), out of slavery and into freedom (Galatians 5.13), out of distress and into peace (1 Corinthians 7.15). According to Paul, therefore, God's call is for all Christians, not just those called to a particular form of ministry in the Church. Nobody is exempted from the imperative to take up the cross and follow Christ and participate in the reconciling ministry of the whole people of God. When Paul, in his letters to the churches at Galatia and Corinth, speaks of those who have been called, he is referring to all the members of the churches there, not simply their leaders. According to Paul, the calling of the people of God is first and foremost rooted in the freedom of God's sovereign grace and not in any human gifts or abilities. Ministry is a gift from God which exists solely to serve God's purposes, not human ends. The Christian vocation is thus a divine calling to serve a divine purpose. Paul's statements concerning God's foreknowledge of those who would respond to this calling merely emphasize God's sole initiative in the Christian vocation:

> We know that all things work together for good for those who love God, *who are called according to his purpose*. For those whom he foreknew he also predestined to be conformed to the image of his Son, in order that he might be the firstborn within a large family. And those whom he predestined he also called; and those whom he called he also justified; and those whom he justified he also glorified. (Romans 8.28–30)

As hard as it is to accept in these modern times, when children as young as 11 and 12 are urged to begin building their *curriculum vitae*, God's call is an act of grace and is not directly related to human merit. It is a calling to 'work together', to 'belong' and to 'be', and for this reason individual Christian vocation is only valid inasmuch as it is an integral part of the vocation of the whole people of God. The Old Testament prophets were called to their personal vocation as prophets and spiritual leaders in order to 'call' Israel to fulfil its divine vocation as the people of God. Their vocation was distinctive but not separate from that of the people they called to on behalf of God. In the same way, the New Testament narrates how what subsequently became the 'permanent' ministries of the Church evolved from the need for practical and distinctive but nonetheless integral ministries, which would enable the *ecclesia* to fulfil its calling and participate in the work of God. The selection of Stephen and the other six deacons as servants of the new community in order to free up the 12 disciples from 'waiting on tables' (Acts 6.1–5) is an illustration of how the shared Christian vocation was differentiated into personal and communal vocations according to the needs of the *ecclesia* so that God's purposes might be fulfilled.

Differentiated or personal vocations are just as dependent on the initiation of God as the communal calling is. Paul writes:

> But when God, who had set me apart before I was born and called me through his grace, was pleased to reveal his Son to me, so that I might proclaim him among the Gentiles. (Galatians 1.15)

Jeremiah similarly narrates how God spoke to him and said:

> Before I formed you in the womb I knew you, and before you were born I consecrated you; I appointed you a prophet to the nations. (Jeremiah 1.5)

Few today, however, are willing to claim as authoritatively as Paul did that God had predestined them to serve as an apostle or an ordained minister of the Church. This leads to the primary dilemma addressed by this chapter: how can either the Church or an individual discern and respond to the initiation of God's calling to a personal vocation within the body of Christ? The next section details how abilities, gifts and charisms have traditionally functioned as a primary means of vocational discernment.

Discerning gifts and graces

In a recent debate among some Methodists about whether a proven ability to preach should be a prerequisite for presbyteral ministry, opinion was divided. Those who were convinced that it was, argued for it on the basis that presbyteral ministry was a ministry of 'word and sacrament' and that it would accordingly be a serious handicap to an effective ministry if the person were unable to preach the word with clarity and conviction. Those who argued against, did so on the grounds that the person concerned might make an outstanding pastor even if they would never become a great preacher, and that the Church needed both forms of ministry. In this, they were able to draw on the support of anecdotal evidence provided by all too many church members in comments such as, 'He can't preach, but he has a lovely manner about him', and 'I can't understand a word she says in the pulpit, but she's always there when you need her.'

The presumption of a direct correlation between ministry and ability was strengthened by the leaders of the Reformation. John Calvin wrote that those who would offer for ordained ministry would first be equipped by God for it:

It is usual also to say, that private men are called to the ministry when they seem fit and apt to discharge it; that is, because learning, conjoined with piety and the other endowments of a good pastor, is a kind of preparation for the office. For those whom the Lord has destined for this great office he previously provides with the armour which is requisite for the discharge of it, that they may not come empty and unprepared.[1]

John Wesley likewise was adamant that those called to the ordained ministry should possess several qualities in order to be able to fulfil the duties of their calling. These he categorized as being either acquired or inherited by grace or nature. The 'natural qualities' he lists in 'An Address to the Clergy' include 'First, a good understanding, a clear apprehension, a sound judgment, and a capacity of reasoning with some closeness.'[2] As might perhaps be expected, given the extent of his own learning, Wesley also deemed 'a competent share of knowledge' of each of the following to be desirable acquired qualities:

Firstly: the office of a minister, 'of the high trust in which he stands, the important work to which he is called'.
Secondly: the Scriptures.
Thirdly: Greek and Hebrew.
Fourthly: history, including ancient customs, chronology and geography.
Fifthly: Some knowledge of the sciences, of logic, metaphysics, at least the general grounds of natural philosophy, as well as of geometry.
Sixthly: the writings of the Church Fathers.
Seventhly: of the world; 'a knowledge of men, of their maxims, tempers, and manners, such as they occur in real life'.[3]

If that were not sufficient, Wesley also expected clergy to have acquired both prudence and 'good breeding', a good voice and 'good delivery both with regard to pronunciation and action'.[4]

Scripturally, however, there is very little support for the idea that fitness for ministry can or should be discerned by an evaluation of existing skills. Paul and Jeremiah were only too aware of their personal inadequacies for the tasks that God had called them to. Paul writes to the Church at Corinth fully aware that others say of him: 'His letters are weighty and strong, but his bodily presence is weak, and his speech contemptible' (2 Corinthians 10.10). Jeremiah similarly has doubts, in his case about his age (Jeremiah 1.6).

Thus, in spite of the presumption of preparedness through the acquisition of 'necessary' intellectual and practical skills, there remained a conviction in the Church that ministry entailed something more. The essential qualities were not those that had been acquired, but those that flow from God's grace:

'For what are all other gifts,' he insisted, 'whether natural or acquired, when compared to the grace of God? And how ought this to animate and govern the whole intention, affection, and practice of a minister of Christ!'[5]

Both Paul and Jeremiah, along with Moses, Amos, Barnabas and many others believed that the Spirit of God would equip them with whatever gifts and graces were necessary for their calling. Personal experience convinced them that God could always overcome or even use their shortcomings (real or perceived) to fulfil their ministry. They knew that it is not human nature, skill or ability, but gift and grace, i.e. *charism*, that forms the prerequisite for ministry.

Trying to discern which *charism* is a prerequisite for which calling and how it is best nurtured and developed is not easy. It is nonetheless essential to correctly identify, affirm and support the gifts of ministry that God is giving to the Church. What the Churches seek is an indication of how the gifts and graces present in the candidate are being called by God into the service of the Church. This naturally presumes that the Church is aware of the nature of the ministry that it needs.

Nowhere is this more evident than in the current policies of the main denominations to recruit, train and ordain for what are being termed 'pioneer' ministries or fresh expressions of Church. The Church of England's 2007 guidelines for the identification, training and deployment of ordained pioneer ministers contains the recommendation that:

Bishops' advisers should watch for candidates who have the necessary vision and gifts to be missionary entrepreneurs: to lead fresh expressions of church and forms of church appropriate to a particular culture . . .

Those who are to advise the bishop in this matter are required to be alert for 'particular experience and a strong track record in pioneering ministries'. The Methodist Church likewise seeks evidence of this specific calling before including the minister (lay or ordained) on an approved list of 'pioneers'. To quote from a recent report:

> The selection process will seek to identify patterns of behaviour (not necessarily in the specific area of beginning fresh expressions) which are focused around entrepreneurial skills. They will include: vision, motivation, the ability to inspire others, understanding of unchurched culture, healthy work/life balance, natural relationship builder, commitment to holistic church growth, responsive to community, utilising the gifts of others, flexibility, team builder, resilient, exercising faith (within the discipline of a 'rule of life'?).[6]

The language of both reports can be interpreted as saying that God will have already equipped the potential candidate with the necessary skills to at least enable this particular vocational calling to be evident.

It would be wrong, however, to deduce from this that the Churches have been leaning towards a more abilities-based or 'functional' understanding of ministerial vocation. Both reports also refer to the fact that pioneer ministry may be a lay as well as ordained vocation. Not all pioneer ministers are called to be ordained. This implies that there is something other than particular skills or practical abilities differentiating between lay and ordained vocations – but what? What is it that will persuade one person with a calling to pioneer ministry in the Church to also believe that they are called to ordained ministry, while convincing another, with (apparently) the same skill set, that they are called to lay ministry: and crucially, how does the Church discern the validity of each?

The Church teaches that ministry is the natural expression of Christian vocation. All Christians, without exception, are called to minister to one another in love in the name of Christ and to share their faith. Not all ministries are open to all Christians, however. A comparison of the answers provided to the World Council of Churches' report *Baptism, Eucharist and Ministry*,[7] suggests that the ability to preside at the sacraments is a specialized form of ministry. Most Churches recognize a twofold vocational structure: the calling and a gifting by God which all Christians share in by virtue of their baptism, and the separate witness and servant structure associated with the ordained vocations. These specialized vocations are servant vocations which evolved out of the need to ensure that the common vocation could be fulfilled.[8]

There is little denominational agreement, however, regarding the initial grounds for differentiating between lay and ordained ministries. Some differentiate on grounds of gender, others on grounds of sexuality. All differentiate to a greater or lesser degree on the grounds of age and academic ability. It is difficult not to see in these grounds evidence of cultural rather than purely theological or spiritual influences. The next section therefore considers the contextual pressures operating on the Church and on an individual seeking to discern the validity of a call to ordained ministry.

Context and conformity in church ministry

Although Christians are advised by Paul to not be conformed to the world (Romans 12.2), the cultural context of each age has played a significant role in establishing the criteria used to differentiate between lay and ordained ministries. The story of the emancipation of women in the Western world, for example, is echoed in the later history of the Church. A hundred years ago it would have been unthinkable for a woman to consider standing for parliament or holding government office. Similarly, women would not have even considered offering for full-time stipendiary parish or circuit ministry. Those women who did believe themselves called to the sacramental, pastoral and preaching ministry by God, often served as missionaries overseas instead where they were able to fulfil at least a part of their calling. The prevailing culture of the day, both socially and ecclesiastically, meant that ordination was simply not an option. The same story could be told of other significant sections of the population such as the poor, the uneducated, the lower class and the immigrant. Conformity to cultural and social expectations has repeatedly shaped theological and spiritual preconceptions, influencing the ability of the Church to discern who is, and who is not, 'suitable' for ordained ministry.

A clear illustration of this can be found in a recent study of Anglican theological training.[9] 'At the beginning of the nineteenth century', notes Dowland, 'it was conventional for clergy of the national Church to be upper-middle or upper-class gentlemen drawn from the public schools and the ancient universities.'[10] Over the course of the century, this changed, assisted by the establishment of 'non-graduate'[11] colleges which were created before synodical bodies were formed and standard vocational examinations existed. By the 1890s, 25 per cent of Anglican clergy had trained in such colleges. Their fathers' occupations ranged from baronet to bootmaker, and the average age of the ordinand in training was between 21 and 23.

This partial opening of the vocation to the priesthood of the Church of England in the nineteenth century needs to be set in its particular context to be properly understood. The population explosion that went hand in hand with the onset of the industrial revolution and the movement into the new cities gave rise to a 'middle class' with professional aspirations. The Church was called to both mission and minister to the rapidly increasing population and managed to do so by drawing on this new class. As Dowland points out, however, this did not meet with universal approval, even from those such as Bickersteth of Ripon who recognized the value of the 'non-graduate' ordinand. 'The education of a theological college is necessarily a class education' he wrote, adding:

> This is the last thing to be desired for the clergy of our Church. If they are really to influence society, if they are really to mould or direct the current of ordinary life not less than in matters of religion, there should be a breadth and depth in their education which the contracted sphere of a Theological College does not permit . . . It is surely a part of our high vocation as ministers of Christ's Church to exercise a wholesome influence on all orders of men and all classes of mind.[12]

In this quote, Bickersteth links the training of the clergy with the change in the role of the parish minister which occurred during the same period. A member of the clergy might previously 'have wielded influence in his local community not only as a minister, but as a local administrator, politician, mainstay of order, and source and organizer of welfare'.[13] By the end of the century, Dowland notes, the role would be far more marginal and would be largely limited to the management of the parish and to the sacerdotal and pastoral duties recognizable as pertaining to the role of the clergy in the twentieth century.

Much more research is needed before it would be safe to conclude that the opening of the Anglican priesthood to non-graduates was either solely or even primarily responsible for the change in the role of parish ministry, but it would similarly be foolish to ignore the strength of the evidence that suggests a link between the two. The more important question from the perspective of this chapter is: what drove the change in the Church's vocational discernment process? Is it really possible that God only began to call non-graduates to the ordained ministry in the nineteenth century, or was it the case that the Church was only able to discern the calling in response to the particular missiological imperative of the time?

A more recent phrasing of the same question asks whether or not God has always called women to the ordained ministry, even though it was only towards the end of the twentieth century that some parts of the Church began to accept the validity of a woman's calling to the ordained ministry. The most contemporary version of the question, of course, directs the Church to consider the calling of homosexual men and women to ordained ministry.

Current partial answers to these questions and the publicity that they have engendered has alerted the general public to the fact that the Church can and does update its selection criteria for testing the call of those exploring a vocation to the ordained ministry. This knowledge has served to encourage the cynical interpretation of a calling to the ordained ministry as something more motivated by cultural and socio-economic pressures than by the work of the Holy Spirit. This interpretation is not new, however; neither is it the preserve of the secular world.

The separation throughout history of the calling to the ordained vocations or offices of the Church from the priesthood of all believers has resulted in the perception, if not the reality, of an ecclesial 'elite' or hierarchy of 'professionals' who are accorded significantly greater respect by virtue of their office. Consequently, such offices have been both highly sought after and protected. The idea of ministry as advancement, as the doorway to a particular position within society, is one of the reasons, although not the primary reason, that all denominations have a process by which a calling to the ordained ministry can and should be tested. It is when that process is changed, or appears to have been circumvented, that concerns about ecclesial accommodation to secular ideals are raised.

Returning to the non-graduates, for example, Bickersteth commented that:

> A larger proportion of the students have been very imperfectly educated to begin with and they resort to the Theological Colleges with the view of qualifying themselves in the cheapest and most expeditious manner to pass the ordination examination.[14]

He may or may not have been right to have been suspicious of their motives, but the fact remains that there were many good secular as well as spiritual reasons for non-graduate students wanting to pass the ordination examination. The status and salary of an ordained minister at that time was often well above that to which a typical non-graduate college student could normally hope to aspire. This was a time of considerable social change, mirroring the shift in emphasis from calling to career in America in the same century when, as Bledstein noted:

A profession no longer circumscribed a man, confining him to a pre-established station in life, including a calling toward which sympathetic parents guided him. A man now actively chose his profession.[15]

A parallel situation occurred in Africa at the turn of the twentieth century just as Africans were beginning to respond to the call to ordained ministry in the wake of earlier Western missionary endeavours. In his recent study of class formation and the professionalization of African clergy, Jack Nelson points out how the Western model of ministry, i.e. full-time professional and stipendiary, as practised by the missionaries, created an expectation of advancement in African ordained ministers that was completely at odds with the gospel that the missionaries were trying to proclaim.[16] Most missionaries were able to build or own their own homes and hire cooks, cleaners and gardeners. They justified doing so on the grounds of the importance of their mission work, in much the same way as the first disciples justified the appointment of the first deacons. As Nelson points out, 'The security of salaried positions that they enjoyed made a deep impression on native peoples.'[17] African converts naturally assumed that this standard of living belonged to all ordained ministers. There was thus a growing ambition among African church pastors and ministers to enjoy the benefits of being a part of the new African professional class which began to emerge in the 1950s. The foreign missionaries became concerned that the lure of status and wealth would lead to a spiritually impoverished Church and so attempted to limit the development of the professional class among their members by controlling the opportunities for education. Although such policies were eventually overturned, they helped to engender a considerable difference between the perceived professional and actual economic status of the ordained clergy in some parts of Africa.

In spite of this, comments Nelson, 'there remain plenty of young students eager to enter the ministry, driven they say by their convictions about the truths of the Christian message'.[18] The suspicion, however, clearly continues in some sections of the population that the calling of clergy may be initiated by a desire for money and status in addition to, rather than solely by, God.

The relationship between the Church and the state was shown by Nelson to have played an important part in the tensions between the 'call' to ministry and the unresolved professional expectations of the African clergy. In an increasingly secular world, the call to ministry is often shaped by an environment that is suspicious or even hostile to its basic intent of participation in the building of the kingdom through service to Christ and the people of God. The call to ministry is, after all, a call to an alternative allegiance which transcends any national or political allegiance. History bears witness to the fact that it is a compelling, at times irrational, call which has often led individuals and the Church into conflict with the state. The change in the relationship between Henry II and Thomas Becket following Becket's ordination is a classic illustration of this.

After a period of relative religious stability in the West, the rise of religious fundamentalism at the close of the twentieth century effectively ended any real, or even perceived, distance between the Church and the state with regard to the vocation of religious professionals. In the United Kingdom and elsewhere, laws against the incitement to religious hatred sit side by side with proposals to increase the provision of chaplains in our prisons, hospitals and armed forces to assist in social cohesion. How can the government ensure that those who undertake such roles do so for the 'right' motives? In a report entitled 'Preventing Extremism Together',[19] the British Government makes it clear that it intends to keep a careful watch on the selection and training programmes for clergy. In the case of imams, the report recommended 'The setting up of a National Resource Unit (NRU) for the development of curricula in madrasah/mosques and Islamic centres.' The NRU will be responsible for developing guidelines for the teaching of staff who function within these institutions. Even though the report insists that such guidelines would be developed 'with respect and in compliance with the diversity and schools of thought in the Muslim Community overall', their 'necessary' existence calls into question the independence of Muslims to follow a particular calling or vocation as an imam. A further recommendation calling for the establishment of continuous professional development programmes 'for the "upskilling" of current imams and mosque officials in the UK' emphasizes the government's concern. Even more disconcerting is the recommendation for 'Theological training to be provided only by specialist Muslim seminaries, Islamic scholars skilled in training imams in the UK and elsewhere for those seeking to pursue further development.'

'Preventing Extremism Together' was written to deal specifically with Islamic extremism but there is no reason to suppose that similar proposals will not eventually be forthcoming for other faiths, including Christianity. Awareness of this places an ever-increasing pressure on the Church to tighten its definition of the religious attributes and levels of professionalism it expects of those it believes are 'called' to serve.

A professional vocation

The current state of religious tension, coupled with the illustrations drawn from nineteenth-century England and twentieth-century Africa, should make it clear that untangling the complex web of socio-economic, cultural and spiritual threads from which the cloth of ordained ministry is spun is not easy, either for the Church or for the individual who believes that they are called to this new way of life. Robert Bellah *et al.* contend that the idea of calling 'has become harder and harder to understand as our society has become more complex and utilitarian and expressive individualism more dominant'.[20] Postmodernity has created a sense of individualistic authority with an emphasis on the self and personal truth which seems to directly contradict the ideals of servanthood and duty implicit in a vocational calling. When coupled with the general loss of altruism and the ascendancy of the cult of the individual as testified to in so-called 'reality TV' programmes like *Big Brother*, it is not difficult to see why what is currently being said of a calling to ordained ministry is also being said of almost all other vocational callings or professions. McKinley expresses it thus:

> We are still told that people are 'called' to the ministry or priesthood but suspect that no God called them. Similarly in the field of law we hear that people are 'called to the bar' although again we know that nobody called them and that the initiative was entirely theirs . . . Since a disproportionate number of those in dominant professions are from families already in or associated with them it would appear whoever's doing the calling, is doing it in a highly biased and self-protective fashion.[21]

Calvin defined the calling to ordained ministry as 'the honest testimony of our heart that we accept the office offered to us, not from ambition or avarice, or any other unlawful motive, but from a sincere fear of God'.[22] It is increasingly difficult, however, in a modern competitive world that places great value on self-serving ambition and personal professional development, to separate calling from career in the Christian ministry. This is not surprising; the practicalities of contemporary ordained ministry mean that ministry is best thought of as a professional career, regardless of how uncomfortable the language sounds. It has all four structural attributes of the professional model as defined by Wilensky[23] in that it is:

1 a full-time occupation, with
2 its own places of training to pass on a specialized set of skills and knowledge base, which is regulated by
3 a formal body which not only sets the standards for practice but also protects the particular monopoly of the clergy in society by ensuring compliance with
4 a code of ethics which clergy themselves enforce.

Similarly, ordained ministry complies with Hall's[24] five attitudinal attributes:

1 It is self-referencing with regard to its practice and beliefs.
2 It offers a unique service to the public in resolving issues which cannot be better resolved without the ordained ministry.
3 It is dependent on a sense of calling to the work.
4 It believes it should be self-regulating.
5 It includes a high degree of personal autonomy.

An individual's calling is not negated by the fact that it is inescapably linked to their cultural and socio-economic context. The fact that the context in which ministry will be conducted can be such a tempting motivation does, however, emphasize the necessity of testing the call. According to Christopherson, clergy are 'modern vocational characters who literally have been called to a career'.[25] Nonetheless, the gracious call of God must be the motivating, compelling, authorizing basis of the candidate's determination to enter into the ordained ministry in exactly the same way that the gracious call of God must lie at the root of any Christian vocation. Unlike other professions which now sit lightly with the notion of call, the question of 'call' is not an option for ministers. It is the only thing that ensures that ministry remains a participation in the responsive work of God rather than a participation in a purely social construct which redefines itself according to its own need to survive.

The rise in the average age of those offering for the ordained ministry means that many who are offering for ministry come equipped with highly professional skills, comparable in their own way with Calvin's and Wesley's list of prerequisites mentioned earlier. Regardless of the age of the person, however, if such gifts are not tempered, shaped and formed by God's gracious call, the person concerned is effectively condemned to 'pursue the secular, rational, professionalized goals of individual careers – careers that draw them into unequal competition with practitioners of modern science-based professions'.[26] This can have several disastrous consequences for both the Church and the individual. In particular, professionalized ministry leads inevitably to the devaluing and de-skilling of the laity. The individualism implicit in professionalized ministry can also lead to an over-emphasis on personal charisms rather than on the gifts and graces of the whole people of God, as indicated in the language of 'my ministry' and 'my Church'. There is perhaps a hint of this problem already surfacing in the early Church during the time of St Paul. In his second letter to the Church at Corinth, Paul writes to justify his own ministry in comparison with that of others, but also to make clear the importance of holding together the diversity of the ministries of the Church. Paul's experiences at Corinth and Galatia indicate the importance of holding on to the unity of all Christian calling and vocation. There may be a twofold structure to the Christian vocation, but the 'call' of God to each is the framework that defines and supports the whole ministry of Christ, both internally within the body of Christ, and externally as Christians participate in the mission of God.

The Church knows that the call of God and the grace which flows from it should be the primary determining factor in the making of ministers from the body of the congregation. Most denominations have historically gone to great lengths to take the genuineness of a call into consideration when determining the suitability or otherwise of a candidate for ministry. In Methodism, for example, those offering for ordained ministry are required to give an account of their call at every stage of their journey to ordination, culminating in a 'testimony service' held just prior to their ordination. It is not the conviction of the 'call' or even its primacy that the Church questions or moderates in the light of the pressures mentioned above, but the process of its discernment. A belief in God's present grace, in the reality of God active in creation, means that the Church cannot dismiss or ignore the context in which ministry takes place and the way in which that inevitably shapes the calling of those who are offering.

The Church is compelled to ask in each generation how the authenticity of the call of God can be determined from amidst competing secular differentiations and specializations. It is in trying to provide an answer to this question that the Church is at greatest risk of misreading the signs of the Spirit and of being too deafened by the clamour of social context to be able to hear the 'still, small whisper' so indicative of God's presence. The signs of the Spirit can easily be confused with the signs of the times, and the still, small whisper is often no more than the person's name. The Church therefore tends to err on the side of caution when attempting to test the call of God to the ministry. This is in spite of the knowledge that Scripture provides countless illustrations of God calling the least obvious candidates to participate in the building of the kingdom. Moses was a murderer, David an adulterer, Paul a persecutor. The history of the Church is similarly littered with an amazing assortment of saints and rebels such as Joan of Arc, Francis of Assisi, Thomas Becket, John Calvin, Martin Luther, John Henry Newman, John Wesley, William and Catherine Booth, each of whom was called of God to minister.

The Church has a dual role to perform in discerning and testing the call of those offering for ordained ministry. On the one hand it must seek to discern the mind of God with regard to the mission and purpose of the whole people of God. Those whom God calls to ministry are often the forerunners or trailblazers of the general direction of the future Church such as Paul and Barnabas. Their ministry, precisely because it is innovative and missional, is often not easy to recognize. The history of the Church is replete with denominations and sects that came into existence because the calling of the minister was not recognized for what it was. On the other hand, the Church is also required to discern the mind of God with regard to those who will build up the whole people of God, such as Stephen and the first deacons. The two roles at first glance appear to be quite distinct, but the fact that Stephen was also the first martyr, and that his martyrdom was as a result of his preaching, should illustrate how they can often overlap.

Trying to discern whether God really has called someone to make new straight paths for the Lord is beset with problems. As has already been noted, passion and religious fervour can all too easily either mask dangerous extremism or be perceived as dangerous to the state; the paths in question may therefore be too politically dangerous and hence pose a threat to the Church's very existence. They may be too economically crooked and endanger the integrity of the Church thereby, and they may be too socially inappropriate and so alienate the very people to whom they are called to proclaim the good news. The difficulties that face the Church in trying to respond with integrity to God's radical mission, while also maintaining internal unity and external credibility with state and society, should not be underestimated. Neither is this problem confined to the more charismatic ministries. There are just as many problems in trying to discern whether God really has called someone to build up the body of Christ in love. The Church is home to some of the world's most vulnerable people, and it is only relatively recently that the Church has recognized and begun to take seriously the extent to which abuse in many forms can be hidden and disguised as pastoralia. The diversity of ministry and of those offering for ministry merely adds to the complexity of the discernment process.

Yet in spite of such difficulties, the Church prayerfully undertakes the task of discerning and testing the call to ministry, not just because Scripture advises it, but because such testing is an integral part of its accountability before God, the people of God and the wider world for its stewardship of the gospel. Ultimately, it is this stewardship that implicitly and explicitly determines the initial grounds for vocational discernment in the Church. Those who are accepted for the ordained ministry of the Church must be able, in the eyes of the Church, to be entrusted with this same stewardship.

Karl Rahner uses the language of hierarchy to clarify this issue. Rather than lay or ordained ministries, he talks in terms of hierarchical and non-hierarchical functions within the Church:

> The hierarchical ministry is exercised *in* the Church and *for* the Church; as far as its purpose and meaning are concerned, it has been designed entirely with a view to the Church and as a function of service to the Church which is the communion of all believers.[27]

In the final section of this chapter, the characteristics of those who are called to this 'hierarchical' or representational form of ministry are explored.

Characteristically called

Those who are called to the ordained ministry as ministers, deacons or priests are called to be representatives of the whole people of God in whom the incarnate power of the gospel is entrusted. The Church of England states:

> Through the lives they lead, priests point to the life of Christ crucified and risen, encouraging all God's people to show love, care and compassion and to strive for justice and peace. As they do this, priests share in people's sorrows and joys as they walk with them on their individual journeys.[28]

When the gospel is lived out in the community, it has the power to transform a community because the gospel is not a narrative about what Jesus did, it is the good news of what Jesus is doing.

It is impossible to embody the gospel without being transformed by it, and a longing for transformation lies at the heart of every calling to ordained ministry. This longing is therefore characteristic of a call to ministry, even though it manifests itself in many different forms. For some, it is the passion for social justice; for others, it is the longing to heal the sick or the need to bind up the broken-hearted. But over and above all such manifestations, it is evident in the deep and personal longing for a lasting and transforming relationship with God. This is the common thread in the lives of all those called to ordained ministry and why it is said that ministers are shaped by their calling. It is as a person begins to respond to the transformation that God is working in their lives through the power of the Holy Spirit that they become more and more conscious of their own calling to participate in the transformation of others. At the same time, they become acutely aware of the fact that this is not something that they feel either well equipped or able to do. And so begins the agonizing processes of trying to make sense of a compulsion to do something that seems utterly impossible and improbable and yet absolutely essential.

A second characteristic of the call to ministry is therefore the very real sense of inadequacy which no professional skill-set can compensate for. The great twentieth-century theologian and pastor Karl Barth is reputed to have written his 13-volume *Church Dogmatics* because he felt unequal to the task of preaching the word of God. Scripture likewise abounds with illustrations of 'inadequate' ministers, from Peter's plea that Jesus leave him, through to Moses, who, in spite of being raised as a son of the princess of Egypt, and presumably educated and trained for leadership, and in spite of the signs and wonders that God enables him to perform, still begs God to 'send someone else' on the grounds that he lacks some essential skill.

Often those who experience a call but who do not respond to it immediately are drawn, as Calvin hints that they might be, to acquire those skills that might assist in the conduct of the duties inherent in the call. Thus a significant portion of those who offer for ordained ministry later in life do so after having first worked in education or social work or in one of the caring professions such as nursing or counselling. Paul's ministry to the gentiles was undoubtedly as effective as it was because of his extensive learning and familiarity with the Roman as well as the Jewish world. It was an essential component of his ministry that he was able to be all things to all people (1 Corinthians 9.22).

The compulsion to pursue the calling, or rather the sense of being pursued by it, is a third characteristic of the calling to ordained ministry. As was noted at the beginning, the call is initiated by God as an act of grace. It is therefore not irresistible, but it can be so compelling that it takes concerted, deliberate effort to deny its claim on life. The story of God's call to

Jonah not only describes the lengths that some will go to in order to try and avoid the call, but also the extraordinary lengths that God is prepared to go to in order that the necessary transformation of the community through God's appointed ministry happens.

It is possible for these three characteristics – the longing, the sense of inadequacy and the compulsion to pursue a calling – to be separately and concomitantly tested by the Church in order to determine the authenticity of an individual's call to ministry. But is that enough? All Christians long for the transformation of the world that only the gospel can realize, yet which they feel compelled to work for. Is there perhaps a further characteristic unique to those called to ordained ministry? According to the Deed of Union of the British Methodist Church:

> Christ's ministers in the church are stewards in the household of God and shepherds of his flock. Some are called and ordained to this sole occupation and have a principal and directing part in these great duties but they hold no priesthood differing in kind from that which is common to all the Lord's people and they have no exclusive title to the preaching of the gospel or the care of souls. These ministries are shared with them by others to whom also the Spirit divides his gifts severally as he wills.[29]

Any unique characteristic of ordained ministry must somehow therefore be related to the concepts of 'sole occupation' and of 'principal and directing part'. Twenty-first-century ministry, however, is often not the sole occupation of those who have been called and ordained. The defining characteristic must accordingly be determined by a willingness to take the principal and directing part in those duties related to the stewardship of the house of God. In this, as in all aspects of ministry, it is Christ who exemplifies the role and defines the standards for leadership expected of those willing to respond to this calling. Christ's leadership led him to both instruct the disciples and to wash their feet. Christ led by example, not by dictate; 'he humbled himself and became obedient to the point of death – even death on a cross' (Philippians 2.8). It was Christ's loving humility, not his great knowledge of Scripture, his ability as a storyteller or his skills as a carpenter, that formed the basis of his charismatic leadership. His love and his compassion for those he was called to lead enabled him to reach out to others and lead them into all truth: truth about themselves, about the world, and about God. The leadership that characterizes the ordained minister therefore is humble, self-sacrificing and obedient. It is a leadership which recognizes the authority of the Church and is obedient to it as that which stands in Christ's stead and which speaks in his name. It is a leadership of care which is communal and inclusive rather than partisan and individualistic.

The care of the sick, the visitation of the housebound, the education of children and the advocacy of the poor and marginalized are the professional domains of a surprising assortment of state-run institutions and volunteer bodies or charities. Many ministers accordingly feel that they have to compete with social workers, teachers, counsellors, youth workers and care assistants for the leadership and oversight of their flock. Not only are they not trained to do this, but the Church is reluctant to give any authority to minister to others in the space that it has ceded to the secular professionals. Modern clergy are repeatedly warned of the dangers of 'interfering' in areas that would once have been considered their sole preserve. But while it might appear that the minister's characteristic pastoral leadership has been usurped by the 'nanny state', this is simply not the case.

The calling to ordained ministry is a calling to take the lead and responsibility for the care of individuals within the wider context of eternity, recognizing their real worth and encouraging them to discover and take up their place as children of God, not just as members of society. It extends past the boundaries of secular care and demands a different form of professionalism, the sort that Christ exemplified through his servant ministry. It is a calling that entails claiming the authority of Scripture and of the Church in such a way that others can be led by example into the presence of God to discover the truth of their identity and so grow in grace and holiness. It is a high calling, which everyone but Christ has fallen short of but which every ordained minister continually aspires to.

Conclusion

All Christian vocations are the gift of God to the people of God for the sake of the gospel. They are reconciling acts of divine grace to which God calls people, as individuals and *ecclesia*, to respond so that they might be made holy. Every call to participate in God's grace is therefore a calling to participate in a ministry which is not dependent on human nature or on human skill. God can and does equip the people of God to fulfil God's purposes; God alone can do this. There are, however, different ministries, and the task of discerning a call to a specific vocation is not simple. The lines of communication from heaven to earth, through which the calling must be heard and authenticated on behalf of the people of God, pass through the Church by the will of God. The Church, as the gathered people of God, is not some faceless institution, but is, as Paul states, the body of Christ with a specific responsibility to proclaim the gospel of the kingdom of God to each generation in such a way that it can be heard.

Stewardship of the gospel has always entailed taking seriously the context in which it needs to be heard. The fact that Christ was male, not female, and that his ministry did not begin until he reached the age of responsible adulthood, was not accidental but was essential to enable the good news to be heard and responded to at that time and in that place. Scripture and history are united in their testimony that context cannot be ignored or dismissed when considering how to communicate a message of vital importance. The determinative contexts, however, are the present and the future, not the past – something that the Church needs to be reminded of. God repeatedly calls ministers to speak to the contemporary context where the gospel needs to be heard. In this generation, as in every previous generation since the time of Christ, this means the existing people of God as well as the unchurched and church-weary. The 'who' is simply those who can be heard.

The desire to safeguard the integrity of the gospel periodically creates in the Church a 'safety deposit box' mentality, in which it is generally mistakenly believed that the fewer people who have the key to unlock it, the better. This is not only contrary to what the gospel teaches, it is also contradicted by the experiential evidence of God's desire for the gospel to be heard, as found in the repeated offers of those who normally lie outside of the accepted criteria for ministry. It often takes both time and courage, however, for the Church to be able to consider ministry that is 'outside of the box'.

For the individual, it often means that the theological language needed to articulate the given focus of ministry does not yet exist. It is helpful at such times to be reminded of the characteristics which all ministries share. The Church has the harder task of ascertaining which of the two forms of ministry, lay or ordained, the focus naturally belongs to. Leadership, governance and oversight change with time, and each new secular model has to be fully evaluated by comparing it to the example set by Christ in the Gospels and in the lives and prayers of the people of God. The Church itself does not call people to ministry, but it naturally finds it easier to discern the call of those whose ministry it is most familiar with and therefore confident of. The calling of God and the discernment of the Church combine best to build up the kingdom when the whole people of God are prepared to participate in the risky example set by Christ's own ministry. Christ was called rabbi, but he was a decidedly unorthodox rabbi who touched the untouchable, communicated with the incommunicable and broke bread with those whom others would consider unclean. He was, by age and gender, lineage and education, orthodox enough to be able to speak. By the power of the Spirit he was also sufficiently different to frustrate the authorities, upset the rulers, and be heard by those who needed to hear him – then as now. The call of God and the tension and frustration that result from God calling people to forms of ministry that the Church is unable to fully recognize is, thank God, by the power of God, always more creative than is initially realized.

Notes

1 John Calvin, *The Institutes of the Christian Religion*, IV:3:11.

2 John Wesley, *The Works of John Wesley*, ed. Thomas Jackson, Grand Rapids: Baker Books, 1979, Vol. 10, p. 482.

3 Jackson, *Works*, Vol. 10, p. 482–5.

4 Jackson, *Works*, Vol. 10, p. 486.

5 Jackson, *Works*, Vol. 10, p. 485.

6 Connexional Fresh Expressions Scheme, Methodist Council Papers, 2007, section 5, http://www.methodistchurch.org.uk/downloads/coun_fe_031007_0777.doc.

7 *Baptism, Eucharist and Ministry*, Geneva: World Council of Churches, 1982.

8 It has been argued, however, that the lack of awareness of the gifting and vocation which all Christians share by the grace of God led at least in part to the way in which the clerical office eventually came to be endowed with final authority over all charisms, effectively subordinating most lay charisms. E. Kilmartin, 'Office and Charism: Reflections on a New Study of Ministry', *Theological Studies*, 83:3, 1977, pp. 547–54.

9 D. Dowland, *Nineteenth-Century Anglican Theological Training: The Redbrick Challenge*, Oxford: Oxford University Press, 1997.

10 Dowland, *Nineteenth-Century*, p. 1.

11 By which is meant colleges created to train ordinands without a degree conferred by Oxford, Cambridge or Durham.

12 Bickersteth of Ripon in 1867, as quoted in Dowland, *Nineteenth-Century*, p. 178.

13 Dowland, *Nineteenth-Century*, p. 178.

14 Charge to the Diocese of Ripon (1876), 8–9, as quoted in Dowland, *Nineteenth-Century*, p. 178.

15 Burton Bledstein, *The Culture of Professionalism: The Middle Class and the Development of Higher Education in America*, New York: W.W. Norton & Co., 1976, quoted in Richard Christopherson, 'Calling and Career in Christian Ministry' in *Review of Religious Research*, 35:3, 1994, pp. 219–37.

16 J. Nelson, 'Class Formation and the Professionalization of an African Clergy', *Journal of Religion in Africa*, 22:2, 1922, pp. 133–51.

17 Nelson, 'Class Formation', pp. 133–51, esp. p. 138.

18 Nelson, 'Class Formation', pp. 133–51, esp. p. 145.

19 'Preventing Extremism Together', working group report, August–October 2005, http://www.communities.gov.uk/archived/general-content/communities/preventingextremismtogether, 2007.

20 Robert Bellah, Robert Madsen, William M. Sullivan, Ann Swidler and Steven M. Tipton, *Habits of the Heart: Individualism and Commitment in American Life*, New York: Harper & Row, 1986.

21 As quoted in Christopherson, *Calling and Career*, pp. 219–37, esp. p. 219.

22 Calvin, *The Institutes of the Christian Religion*, IV:3:11.

23 Harold L. Wilensky, 'The Professionalization of Everyone?', *American Journal of Sociology*, 70, 1964, pp. 137–58.

24 Richard H. Hall, 'Professionalization and Bureaucratization', *American Sociological Reiew*, 33, 1968, pp. 92–103.

25 Christopherson, 'Calling and Career', pp. 219–37.

26 Christopherson, 'Calling and Career', pp. 219–37, esp. p. 222.

27 Karl Rahner, *Theological Investigations Vol. II: Man in the Church*, London: Darton, Longman & Todd, 1963, p. 330.

28 http://www.cofe.anglican.org/lifeevents/ministry/ministryinthecofe/ministryincofe.html/#criteria, December 2007.

29 Methodist Church, *The Constitutional Practice and Discipline of the Methodist Church*, Vol. II, Part I, Deed of Union, Peterborough: Methodist Publishing House, 2007.

A Model of Ministerial Formation:
Conceptual Framework and Practical Implications[1]

JEREMY WORTHEN

Introduction: after the Victorians

It would be simplistic but not perhaps entirely misleading to characterize the situation of the Anglican and Free Churches in England at the start of the twenty-first century as still to a large extent conditioned by the slow unravelling of cultural and social patterns that took decisive shape in the Victorian period, with a consequent hesitation between the search for new paradigms on the one hand and the desire to preserve a still substantial legacy on the other. Arguably, approaches to preparation for ministry are a case in point. It was only in the nineteenth century that the Church of England began to create specialized institutions for ministerial education, the task of preparing its future clergy having previously resided with Oxford and Cambridge Universities.[2] Partly because of their exclusion from the universities in the preceding period, Free Churches had developed some training institutions of their own in the eighteenth century, but they too in the age of Queen Victoria were keen to build special colleges for training clergy in cities of historic and academic significance. Until the 1960s, this aspect of the Victorian legacy was not widely questioned in mainstream debate. Yet today it seems increasingly precarious. Should we lament – or rejoice?

A number of factors have sharpened the question about whether this particular Victorian pattern – studying in residence for a sustained period of time at a specialized church institution as the normal way of preparing for ordained ministry, to be followed (at least in the Church of England) by something like a professional apprenticeship – can indeed continue to serve the contemporary Church. We might sum up the issue here, however, as being about the extent to which such studying and training are best done in an institutional context that is located apart from the ordinary, ongoing life of the Church in the world. If ministry itself is now seen as essentially collaborative (in terms of the Church) and contextual (in relation to the world), surely it is not best prepared for by a prolonged period of removal from both the ordinary life of the Church, with its rich texture of lay as well as ordained ministries, and from the ongoing flow of social and cultural life, in order to be wholly immersed in an environment focused on the goal of ordained ministry (and therefore to some extent inevitably academic, clerical and ecclesiastical). The interrelated phenomena of the growth of lay ministries and of focused training for them, the development of self-supporting forms of ordained ministry, the rise of provision for ministerial education through part-time study, and the advocacy of contextual approaches to theology itself are all relevant as part of the background here.

The other factor that has thrown doubt on the continuing viability of the pattern of ministerial training inherited from the Victorians is finance. Sustaining the institutional environments that allow those preparing for ordained ministry in particular to study and learn residentially in a primary location that is not simply part of a university, local church or national or regional training department is inevitably very costly – and indeed the price has risen considerably, since those undertaking it have become much more likely to have responsibilities for dependent children. Of course, one can ask such institutions to diversify as the price of their continued existence (as has increasingly happened across the board over the last few decades), but that simply brings us back to the fundamental question of whether a certain kind of detachment from university, congregation and regional and national church structures is appropriate or not in preparing for ministry. The response to that question, made more or less reflectively, has inevitably been decisive for the development of institutions providing training through part-time study since their inception in the 1960s. To what extent should they be seeking to replicate something of the 'apartness' of the Victorian model (with its roots much further back in the post-Tridentine Roman Catholic seminary) in the experience of their students? Or should they be seizing the opportunity to relegate this model to a now irrelevant past in the name of a more thoroughly collaborative and contextual present day?

These are matters of some urgency in the current context: allocation of scarce resources is likely to determine in the coming decades just how this part of the Victorian legacy finally unravels. Yet there also needs to be some careful thinking about what it is that the Churches want to achieve through the resources they commit to initial ministerial education, and how such aims relate to concrete patterns of learning. What provides the linkage between such areas of consideration is a model of ministerial formation. Inevitably, there will be a plurality of such models – in official reports and documents, in the minds of church leaders and theological educators, and in the actual experience of students. Such models may in fact be disparate and even contradictory, while remaining in many cases unacknowledged or at the very least unexposed to critical scrutiny by others involved in this enterprise. This chapter is intended to help foster thoughtful discussion of the relationship between theology, educational practice and priorities for limited resources by proposing a possible model for understanding ministerial formation. The model is set out in the three sections that follow, with some practical implications for the Churches' response to the continuing erosion of the Victorian pattern being identified in the conclusion. My hope would be that this chapter, based on the situation of the Anglican and (to a lesser extent) Free Churches in England, may be of some value to people engaged with such discussions at various levels – as church leaders, educators, clergy, students, members of bodies with budgetary powers – in this country and elsewhere.

Formation and professional vocation

Formation has become increasingly common as a central term in public discourse within the Churches about preparation for ministry. A recent, substantial report within the Church of England on ministerial education had as its main title *Formation for Ministry Within a Learning Church*,[3] while the relevant national department of the Methodist Church is called Formation in Ministry. At one level, it is perhaps a sign of fruitful ecumenical exchange that a term with origins in Catholic traditions of Christianity should now be so widely accepted. Yet it could also be argued that the current prevalence of formation as a concept to some extent disguises deeper disagreements under the appearance of consensus. Most people involved agree that preparation for ministry requires something more than the acquisition of the requisite knowledge and skills to exercise ministerial tasks competently – something more, therefore, than 'training' understood in a minimal way, and something more too than the kind of enhancement of knowledge and skills that can be assessed within the kind of higher education frameworks that are now more or less ubiquitous in clergy training in this country. Talking about formation is undoubtedly a valuable way to name that further dimension. But what is the nature of that 'more than'? It is not clear that there is at this point substantial consensus on the answer, and it is therefore not helpful for the concept of formation to be deployed in a way that implies that such consensus actually exists. Moreover, given that the rationale for distinctive institutions for ministerial preparation – in the face of the kind of questioning sketched in the introductory section – is increasingly likely to be articulated in terms of the distinctiveness of ministerial formation, clarity is vital for an informed debate about the survival and development of such institutions.

First, then, I would like to offer a preliminary account of what broad area we are talking about when we use the term 'formation' in a vocational context. I would suggest that formation is something that follows from and prepares for a vocation that cannot be immediately achieved and therefore requires some sort of process of change and adjustment in order for the person who receives that vocation to be able to realize it. That process is what we mean by formation. Second, I would like to sketch out two types of formation that are in different ways appealed to in discussions of ministerial formation: professional formation (in this section) and (in the following section) spiritual formation.

Given that there is a common understanding within our culture of particular professions as vocations that cannot be immediately lived out by someone who identifies with one of them as 'their' vocation, it is perfectly understandable that we should speak about the process by which someone prepares to realize such a vocation to such a role as their professional formation. The 'professional' in modern society is not simply someone trained to discharge a particular range of tasks, but someone who has an awareness of the expectations that accompany the designated role on the part of colleagues and of the public, and who is able to negotiate these expectations on the basis of certain attitudes and values that have come to be associated with the role and the way in which individuals who inhabit it address the concrete tasks associated with it. There is an ethical dimension, therefore, as well as an academic and technical one, to professional formation.[4] Nor is this simply a matter of learning a given code of practice, although of course that is also important. Being a professional requires that the person has become familiar with some relatively intangible traditions, through awareness of both past history and present reality focused on exemplary members of the profession. It also requires assimilation of certain traits of behaviour, at least as long as the person is acting within the role. To sum up, becoming any kind of professional, not just an ordained minister, involves something more than the acquisition of formally assessable knowledge and skills. It requires a complex process of internalization of understanding and attitudes that is related to but cannot be simply reduced to formal study and training focused on particular tasks. We can call this process, as one that follows from and prepares for a vocation to a particular professional vocation, professional formation.

Now, one way to conceive of ministerial formation is simply as a specific instance of professional formation. Indeed, when influential figures in the Victorian Churches urged the founding of residential colleges for ordination training, they were only following the lead of other emerging professions, for whom the development of such institutions was a key element in fostering a professional identity.[5] Insofar as the Churches today wish ordained ministry to remain to any extent at all a recognized profession, professional formation of some kind is clearly essential. The corollary of this is that when church leaders systematically reduce or occasionally waive for particular individuals the normal requirements for ministerial formation, they are undermining the ability of all clergy, whatever their training, to inhabit a recognized role as professionals within contemporary society, because part of the trust invested in any professional is the assumption that they have not only acquired certain skills and the capacity to deploy relevant knowledge but that they share some common frame of outlook and attitudes arising from a basic consistency in professional formation. Clergy, like other professionals, need to be able to negotiate a complex set of cultural expectations on the basis of internalized understanding and values. For them, as for other professionals, mentoring, peer relations and familiarity with a range of role models will be essential in the formational process, as well as academic study and opportunities for supervised practice. There will need to be careful attention from those overseeing their development to the way that they do things and the kind of attitudes that they communicate in their activity, as well as to questions of basic competence.

A rather quaint, but admirably direct, passage from the 1913 edition of the *Catholic Encyclopedia* expresses this very clearly in its section on 'The Purpose of Seminary Education' for someone who wants to be a priest: 'like an army or navy officer, he needs to acquire the manners and personal habits becoming his calling'.[6] Despite its appearance as the first word of the report's title, the much more recent Church of England document, *Formation for Ministry Within a Learning Church*, has only a relatively brief section on the concept of formation, which does, however, include an insistence that ministerial formation means participation 'in a process of being conformed to the public role' of the minister, conceived as including prayer, 'acting as a spokesperson on behalf of and to the Church', continued growth in learning and 'leadership of the Christian community'.[7] No clear explication is given of exactly what is involved in conformity to the public role thus described, but the context suggests that it is precisely the kind of professional formation that has just been set out that the report's authors have in mind at this point. The reasons why, at the start of the twenty-first century people are likely to be less confident about delineating 'the manners and personal habits' of the clergy in Anglican and Free Church contexts than they might have been in the Edwardian age, would include the prevalence of self-supporting forms of ordained ministry that mean it may well not be the only profession a person is exercising, as well as a wider reluctance to prescribe uniformity in the face of cultural diversity. One might also argue with some cogency, however, that precisely these factors make appropriately sensitive professional formation all the more important if ministers are to be able to function within a context of effective recognition and indeed continued acceptance within both the Churches and wider society.

Formation and spiritual vocation

The two very different sources referred to in the paragraph above make it clear that professional formation alone is not all that is relevant here: there is also a need to recognize the spiritual dimension of the process, a dimension which needs to be accounted for in explicitly theological terms. Thus *Formation for Ministry Within a Learning Church* juxtaposes the 'process of being conformed to the public role' with 'elements of transformation, the Spirit of God at work in fallible human beings, *forming* Christ in them'. The 1913 *Catholic Encyclopedia* does not in fact use 'formation' in an inclusive sense to refer to the preparation of men for priestly ministry, in contrast with, for example, the Vatican II Decree *Optatam totius*; instead, it invariably qualifies formation as, for example, 'character-formation,' 'moral and religious formation' or (most frequently), 'spiritual formation'.[8] A publication from the World Council of Churches specifically addresses the question of how spiritual formation is to be properly integrated with education and training in the making of ministers.[9] Here again, however, if progress is to be made in understanding, it is important to be clear what we mean by the critical terms being used.

Now, at one level it is evident – and perhaps more evident to us than to our forebears a century ago – that spiritual formation is something that pertains to every baptized person. If formation follows from and prepares for a vocation that cannot be immediately embraced in its totality, then it is certainly necessary for our response to our vocation to life in the Spirit through Christ. Romans 8.28 speaks of all things working together for good for those 'who are called according to his purpose', with Romans 8.29 then explicating this purpose in terms of becoming 'conformed [*summorphous*] to the image of his Son'. The use of terms relating

to the verb *morphoo*, 'to form', in Paul conveys the reality that to be
called in Christ is to be engaged in a process of dynamic change in order
to say 'Yes' to that call with the whole of our being. We might note a
partial contrast here with the Hebrew Bible, where God's 'forming' tends
to be spoken of via analogy with either the manufacture of artefacts or
biological birth (with two distinct roots for these), but in either case with
reference to something 'done' – a past event. In Galatians 4.19, on the
other hand, Paul uses the language of birth to say that he suffers labour
pains 'until Christ is formed [*morphothei*] in you' – clearly a process that
is not yet complete but still unfolding in the present moment. Similarly,
Romans 8.28–30 as a whole indicates that the formation of Christians,
as a 'conformation' to the likeness of Christ that follows from our
vocation to life in him crucified and risen and prepares us for the fullness
of that life at the resurrection of the dead, is something that is being
worked out in the midst of the difficulties and uncertainties of our mortal
time.

Spiritual formation, then, is something that takes time, specifically the
time given to us between the resurrection of the crucified Christ and our
resurrection with him at the end of time, and that is defined in terms of
becoming like the Lord Jesus Christ (cf. also Philippians 3.10). Paul's use
of the prefix *meta-* in some passages underlines that such conformation is
also transformation: that it is not simply a case of 'development' or evo-
lution from where we are, but needs to be understood as change that is
more radical, leaving no part of who we are untouched. So, for instance,
at the end of 2 Corinthians 3, he writes that we who gaze on the Lord 'are
being transformed [*metamorphoumetha*] . . . from glory to glory' (2
Corinthians 3.18). The idea that in perception, whose paradigm is vision,
there is a process of assimilation of the perceiver to what is perceived, is a
commonplace of pre-modern thought, reflected also for instance in the
assertion of 1 John 3.2 that 'when he is revealed, we will be like him, for
we will see him as he is', but in the New Testament this idea intersects
with an eschatological perspective in which what we are assimilated to is
life beyond death – resurrection – which embraces the discontinuity of
death within its affirmation of eternal life. Ultimately, the Western
Christian tradition will come to interpret this teaching from its sources
through the relationship between what is given in human nature and what
is beyond that human nature: what is given to human beings specifically *is*
a horizon of openness to what is not given but beyond them – the eternal
life of God, who is truth, beauty, goodness and all perfection. We do not
possess the means to attain the horizon for which we naturally reach, but
must wait for the transforming revelation of God, the 'new' Word that

comes to us as something transcending all our expectation while also enabling us to touch what lies beyond it.[10]

So how might we begin to describe such spiritual formation, given that it may be characterized as both a conformation to Christ and as a transformation of our given nature which transfigures it to redeem it for its predestined purpose? In Romans 12.2, Paul exhorts his readers, 'Do not be conformed to [*suschematizesthe*] this world, but be transformed [*metamorphousthe*] by the renewing [*anakainosei*] of your minds, so that you may discern what is the will of God – what is good and acceptable and perfect.' In the final part of this section, I would like to draw briefly on Augustine, and in particular the latter part of the *De trinitate*, to offer a very rough sketch of what such a 'renewing' or 'making new' of our minds might mean, as one way of explicating the process of spiritual formation.

Augustine describes the image of God as residing in the human mind, and specifically in the complex interrelationship between remembering, understanding and willing that is constitutive of our mental life. While this image is at the deepest level inextricable for Augustine from our being human, it is realized as likeness only insofar as our minds are turned towards God as the ground and the end of our life, so that our remembrance is pervaded with the awareness of God and God's action, our understanding is rooted in and reaches out for the limitless divine wisdom, and our willing is a participation in the love of God that has been poured into our hearts through the Holy Spirit. Augustine, as he faithfully seeks for understanding of what is given in the Church's faith, is trying to outline the process by which we are 'transformed by the renewing of our minds' – by engaging in the interpretation of Scripture while also drawing critically from other cultural traditions of wisdom about human being (in his case, specifically ancient philosophy), as well as bearing witness to his own experience of the work of grace with the concomitant struggle to make sense of this that is dramatized so powerfully in the *Confessions*. So, for instance, Augustine acknowledges the 'two-dimensional' reality of human being as soul and body, physical and that which is transcending the limits of our physicality, yet both bound together and neither ultimately independent from the other. We are fragile and multi-layered beings by our created nature, and since the fall those delicate dynamics, interior and social, are fraught with the destructive urges of sin (*concupiscentia*), which militate against any kind of 'turning' of the soul towards God so that its image may be fulfilled in likeness. He is acutely conscious of the complex, indeed ultimately unfathomable, processes that are bound up with our remembering, understanding and willing, and has a broader case to make (in the context of the Pelagian controversy) that in order for these to embrace their divine ground as their conscious object, there needs to take place a miracle of grace that we cannot demand or control, nor measure and possess – one that takes a lifetime and beyond in order to 'work all things together for good' to the achievement of God's purpose for us of conformity to the beloved Son.

Our thinking about spiritual formation today will properly draw on the interpretation of Scripture and the philosophical and psychological approaches current in our own time, as well as the contribution of Augustine and others to the Christian tradition, yet Augustine's schema can still serve as a useful point of departure for our contemporary reflection. God commands us to 'remember' who we are in relation to God – God's creation, the object of God's love, addressed by God with a call that desires a response. As Augustine already saw, and psychodynamic models have underlined in their own idiom, memory is a multi-stranded activity in which there is a necessary dialectic between the accessible and the inaccessible. Therefore the call to remember – to be mindful – of God and of ourselves before God is not one that can be immediately followed in its totality; it requires a process of formation, under the hand of God. Next, God wants us to understand, to be advancing in knowledge towards full maturity in Christ, the wisdom of God: to understand ourselves, the world, the Triune God, all in relation to one another. Responding to this call, also, is not a straightforward matter for immediate achievement: personal, cultural and social factors combine to constrain our drive for understanding and to bind us in limited and ultimately sinful habits of explanation. Again, formation is required if we are to embrace God's summons. Finally, God calls us to love – to love God with the whole of our complex and multilayered self in unity, and to love our neighbour as ourselves. So that we might respond to this call, the Father sends us the Spirit through the Son. However, welcoming the Spirit into our hearts so that we may dwell in God and God in us, our lives will be transformed so that we can come 'to discern the will of God – what is good and holy and perfect'; and we will meet constant resistance from inside and outside ourselves for the duration of our mortal lives. Our deepest 'wound' is the fragmentation of our will, its lack of focus in the limitless love of God, such that even when we think we are willing our soul's healing we are always also wanting to cling onto the addictive traces of its sickness. Over time, our time, the divine healer can work on that wound, by the intertwining of grace which arouses desire and our desiring invocation for the fullness of grace. Through all of this, our minds are made new so that we can be transformed into the likeness of Christ, the Word and Wisdom of God.

The distinctiveness of ministerial formation

Given the opening thesis that formation follows from and prepares for vocation, the pivotal question for explicating the distinctiveness of ministerial formation has to be the character of ministerial vocation itself. For a person of faith to consider that they are called to ordained ministry is to open themselves to a vocation that is professional (to some extent) in definition and to be lived out in the context of their ongoing spiritual formation. It should therefore be evident that ministerial formation must include professional formation as well as the kind of continuing attention to spiritual formation that is proper to all Christians. Indeed, if it is accepted, as many ordination liturgies indicate, that ordained ministers are called to be exemplary in their Christian discipleship, then it is completely fitting that there should be particularly close attention given to spiritual formation in the course of preparation for and subsequent reflection on ordination within the life of the Church. Still, we might also note that any Christian who decides to accept a professional vocation will not only need to engage in the relevant professional formation but also be attentive to the relationship between such formation and their continuing spiritual formation. To that extent, the fact that professional formation needs to be related to spiritual formation does not provide for a very clear account of the distinctiveness of ministerial formation in the case of those called to orders.

In this section, I would like to propose something more than this, however. For it seems to me to be at least implicit in the practice of setting people aside for a lifelong order of ministry (a practice continued by Anglican and historic Protestant Churches from the early centuries of Christianity) that such orders are themselves gifts of the Spirit to the Church, and not only 'professions' to be exercised in conjunction with the continuation of the individual's spiritual life. The notion of such orders as a gift is an important one both for comprehending the perseverance of the Church in contexts where such orders have been interrupted and for underlining the importance of spiritual discernment, not just professional assessment, in deciding whether or not a person is called to such an office. A gift is freely given, and therefore a vocation to ordination does not follow automatically from having particular skills and qualities, or even from the need of the Church for people to fulfil certain roles. Gifts share in the mystery of freedom, divine and human: God's freedom to offer, our freedom to refuse. Moreover, this is a gift to be received for the rest of one's life: to accept it is to make in public lifelong vows and promises, the nearest parallel to which for most people will be marriage, which may itself be helpfully understood as a vocation. Analogously to marriage, the vocation to a lifelong order of ministry is integrative, in that it serves as a point of integration for all aspects of one's life, rather than being confined in its influence to a particular part of it. After ordination, there will never be a context where a person can put their ministerial calling to one side and act again simply as a lay Christian, just as after marriage a person cannot sometimes decide to be for a while a single person again. All that they do in the service of Christ will be done for example as a priest, presbyter, deacon, minister of word and sacraments. They will carry on doing many of the same things as before – but somehow the way they do them will shift, as the vocation to a particular order shapes every aspect of their continuing discipleship.

To continue the analogy with marriage, a vocation to an order of ministry is a call to specific responsibility, and as such brings an increase of both authority and accountability, which in human experience will mean a changing dialectic of power and autonomy. Ordained persons receive authority to do certain things which lay people ordinarily do not, but they are also accountable in ways that lay people ordinarily are not. They will have opportunities to shape the life of congregations, to exercise the power of influence and sometimes of compulsion or refusal. Yet they will also, in crucial respects, lose freedoms: the freedom to move congregations within a denomination without consultation, the freedom to move between denominations in search of spiritual growth, and the freedom to criticize aspects of the life of one's Church or refuse to abide by its instruction without fear of disciplinary action or (in some cases) adverse impact on their financial security and prospects for future work. Beyond all such specific points, however, which will clearly vary depending on one's denomination and to a certain extent on the prevailing culture at local and national level, to accept a vocation to such responsibility is to commit oneself to sustaining what might be called a pastoral mentality. Just as the married person must always bear in mind the question, 'How will this affect my spouse?', so the ordained person must always be thinking about the question, 'How will this affect the Church?' – and not just the Church catholic and apostolic, but the particular Church to which I am called and licensed. And to carry that question continually in one's heart is to engage in a kind of self-limitation that marks the 'character' of the ordained person as distinctive: not holier or better than the non-ordained among the people of God, but configured by a particular focus of responsibility with which they are entrusted by that people, for that people.

In the light of these reflections on the vocation to ordained ministry, therefore, it is clear that to be called to such a ministry is to receive a vocation that is *both* professional *and* spiritual, not simply professional but linked to the spiritual vocation of all baptized Christians. And if that is how we should understand ministerial vocation, our conception of ministerial formation needs to flow from this. Ministerial vocation, then, needs to bring together professional and spiritual formation, not as two separate activities, but as two interrelating dimensions of a single process. It is a professional vocation that is bound to be determinative for the spiritual formation of those who embrace it, and a spiritual vocation that has to be anchored in the concrete responsibilities of a professional role and therefore prepared for by professional formation. Ministerial formation, therefore, requires the coming together of the two types of formation already described in dynamic interaction.

We might briefly explore this further by reference again to Augustine's outline of the journey of spiritual formation as the restoration of the divine image in the human mind through the (re)turning of remembering, knowing and willing/loving to their ground and end – God – as their conscious and primary object. To do this, I would also like to suggest a possible correlation between Augustine's mental trinity and what are sometimes spoken of as three dimensions of any process of growth in learning: being, knowing and doing. For instance, to believe that I am called to ordination is to narrate my life story in a particular way, so that this transition to a professional role becomes a pivotal point within it. How will such a narration affect my primary sense of spiritual narrative – of how grace has been at work in my life and how I have responded to it? There are two opposite dangers here, it might be suggested. On the one hand, my sense of 'being' before God as held through my memory may remain somehow insulated from the vocation to ordained ministry, so that, for example, I sense a gap between living out this vocation and meeting 'my spiritual needs', or I struggle to inhabit ministerial roles as something other than an externalized set of expectations and demands. On the other hand, my spiritual 'being' may become so wholly absorbed in my professional 'being' as a member of the clergy that I start to find it increasingly difficult to attend to and rejoice in the presence of the living God except when exercising publicly recognized clerical roles and related forms of activity. The transformation associated with 'remembering' in Augustine, then, can be related to the challenges of growth in 'being' for ministerial formation.

In the case of 'knowing' as one dimension of formation that relates in particular to Augustine's point of 'understanding', some parallel issues might be noted. In order to meet the professional demands of being an ordained minister, I need to attain a good basic grasp of Christian theology as an academic discipline, and draw on this to reflect on ministerial practice, including worship and prayer. Once again, I can resist any real integration of the professional and the spiritual and ensure that my advances in academic study in the classroom and my growth in spiritual understanding in the chapel run on separate tracks. Yet it can also be the case that students become so immersed in professionally orientated study that it displaces any sustained engagement with seeking to know the Trinity through the Son with the Spirit. Knowing 'how to' lead worship, pray and guide others in their spiritual journey can appear to work against giving oneself over to worship, prayer and one's own unrepeatable journey towards union with God. Once again, ministerial formation needs to face such difficulties clearly and foster a positive interchange between progress in academic and practical 'knowing' on the one hand and growth in spiritual 'understanding' on the other.

Finally, in the case of Augustine's 'willing', choosing to accept this professional and spiritual vocation focused on pastoral responsibility is inevitably likely to generate a complex interaction of eagerness and resistance from the particular person – complex because human beings are multidimensional creatures, with the dialectic of conscious and unconscious processes being constitutive of our selfhood, and because we are sinful creatures in whom the will for what is good is constantly being subverted so that it tends towards the less good and the evil. It is one thing to train people effectively in 'doing' certain tasks, like leading worship, preaching, teaching, exercising leadership of congregations and sharing the good news of Christ. Yet in order to do these things as part of a spiritual vocation, my motivations for doing them, indeed my motivations in play while doing them, need to be carefully considered. When I do them, is my will at one in love with the will of the Lord; and if not, what may be the obstacles in growing towards the point of such union with him? The goal has to be that I will the whole of what belongs to this vocation with the whole of my heart, because that heart is set on the things of God and I believe that this vocation is God's gift for me. Yet the shifting constellation of power and autonomy that we have seen to be bound up with transition to ordained ministry precipitates conflicting emotional responses – conflicting with each other and also with conscious goals and values.[11] How 'whole' is my will to do that to which I and the Church believe I am called as an ordained minister? These are the kind of questions that belong in a specific way to the process of ministerial formation on the model that is being proposed and which will need to find appropriate space for sustained attention within the contexts provided for it.

Conclusion: communities of ministerial formation

This chapter has sought to outline a distinctive model of ministerial formation specifically in the case of people with a vocation to ordained ministry, though there might well also be applications to other forms of Christian vocation. It has been argued that such a vocation, because it is both professional and spiritual in its basic character, requires a process of formation that is both professional and spiritual. This means a properly rigorous professional formation, and careful attention to spiritual formation as an integral part of the unfolding experience of every baptized person; but it also requires something more than this. It requires a context in which the intricate dialogue that is bound to emerge between the two trajectories of professional and spiritual formation can be supported and fostered, for without such a dialogue there are profound dangers for the sustaining of a fruitful vocation over the lifetime that the gift of orders demands from those who receive it.

Yet, what would it mean for such a dialogue to be 'supported and fostered'? Clearly this can be – and indeed in any case needs to be – done in a variety of ways, across formational contexts ranging from relative detachment from the ongoing practice of ministry to direct engagement in it. But the creation of communities of ministerial formation is likely to be integral to achieving this. What I mean by such a community is a group of people who meet together regularly and develop a sense of mutual belonging focused on the shared and profoundly challenging task of ministerial formation as here defined. That requires them to hold in common a commitment to spiritual formation and a commitment to the professional formation of the clergy in its fullness, including the challenges of academic theology and of practical engagement. Such a community will be primarily differentiated between those who hold the responsibility for ensuring the community is properly focused on its goals and has the resources to meet them, and those who are consciously engaging in the process of ministerial formation. The fostering of dialogue will require from the staff who 'frame' it a high collective level of expertise in academic theology and practical ministry, a profound and evident commitment to the spiritual journey and an attentive care for their students such that they are able to enter and indeed provoke the kind of dialogue between professional and spiritual formation that was described in the previous section. It will require from students a willingness to engage wholeheartedly with the challenges of professional formation while also continuing to seek spiritual and personal growth, together with the recognition that these interior tasks are best advanced in the context of relationships of trust with those who are also committed to them – both fellow students and staff – relationships that will take time and care to nourish. Such communities will naturally find their primary framework to be shared worship, including sacramental worship. They will practise the virtue of hospitality and seek to share with others outside this particular community the resources that they require to exist and continue to generate, without losing their particular defining focus in ministerial formation. Finally, they will recognize that they are liminal communities, communities of transition and not permanent homes for any of those involved. They exist for the sake of something else: the living out of ordained vocations in the Church, for love of the world in the service of Christ. As liminal communities, they are likely to generate a certain intensity in interpersonal relationships, but they also should be conscious that this is the intensity associated with what Victor Turner called 'communitas' by way of contrast with the relatedness we find within the ordinary, ongoing structures of human life.[12]

These final reflections suggest a need for careful distinctions in response to the pressing questions with which the contemporary Churches are grappling about provision for ministerial education, as discussed in the opening section of the chapter. The Victorian pattern certainly has no kind of theological warrant to remain the paradigm for such education in perpetuity, with all other forms of preparation for ministry – such as part-time courses – being viewed as poor relations. Yet there also needs to be appropriate resistance to the idea that ministerial education is something that can be somehow readily 'fitted onto' institutional contexts that are primarily intended to meet quite different needs, or that it can be readily broken down into a series of constituent tasks with each to be then put out to independent tender for the lowest bid. If there is to be more than lip service paid to the concept of ministerial formation, then there has to be a commitment to creating and sustaining communities of ministerial formation as described in the previous paragraph. Such communities can exist in residential and part-time settings, although of course they will have a different character in each case. They can be part of the experience of students who are preparing for public ministry, and of those who have now entered it but remain in a 'formative', initial phase and are deemed to be still in a process of education for full ministerial responsibility (for example, curates in the Church of England, or probationer ministers in Methodism).

Such communities need not involve independent residential institutions – although the strengths of such institutions for sustaining them should not be underestimated – but they will nonetheless be costly for the

Churches and for those who belong to them. They will be costly in terms of time, for bringing together people who share this purpose in such a way that appropriate relationships can grow, between staff and students and between the students themselves, will take time that might *prima facie* be thought better spent in studying or praying individually or in 'getting on with the job' of ministry. It will cost time that cannot be 'accounted' for according to the contract model that is now the official ideology of ministerial training in many Churches as well as higher education in the UK: institutions receive a budget in return for 'guaranteeing' certain outcomes in terms of students' performance post-completion. Yet spiritual formation is the work of the free Spirit of the sovereign God, who asks us to wait, to be still, to listen, without signing a contract about the assessable benefits that will accrue from such apparent inactivity. The contract model presumes we know – indeed ought to know before parting with our money – exactly what we are purchasing. The fruits of ministerial formation as set out in the previous section, however, can only be predicted to be surprising for those who really seek them.

Sustaining communities that can support and foster the dialogue at the heart of ministerial formation will also be costly in terms of personnel, for the qualities required of the staff who hold responsibility for such communities as set out above are not a combination that is easily found. There needs to be a strategy for drawing people in who have the gifts for this work, keeping them engaged while their potential is developed appropriately and then ensuring they can make choices about whether this work is their own particular vocation in the longer term. It should go without saying that the smaller the number of staff who hold such responsibility, the heavier the demands that will inevitably be placed upon them in terms of awareness of and engagement with all the complex dimensions of ministerial formation if they are to be able to discharge that responsibility effectively. Finally, the extent to which such communities of formation have institutional independence of, for example, higher education institutions or church bodies, is basically a pragmatic one. The ideal of separate institutions is part of the Victorian legacy that may – or may not – be quietly buried in the decades to come. The Victorians grasped, however, that in the modern age in particular, in which we still live, whatever words we use to qualify the adjective, ordained ministers needed a thorough professional formation in a context that took seriously spiritual formation, and that developing distinctive communities of formation was integral to this process. For that we should be grateful, and part of that gratitude should be a concern to ensure we do not thoughtlessly squander what they carefully gathered to bequeath to us in this regard.

Notes

1 I am grateful to staff and students at the South East Institute for Theological Education with whom I have discussed education, training and formation for Christian ministry over the past decade. I am particularly appreciative of comments made by Justine Allain Chapman, Nick Townsend and Mark Wakelin in response to an initial presentation of the key ideas for this chapter.

2 Owen Chadwick, *The Founding of Cuddesdon*, Oxford: Charles Batey, 1954, pp. 1–9.

3 *Formation for Ministry Within a Learning Church: The Report of the Working Party for the Structure and Funding of Ordination Training (SFOT)*, GS 1496, London: Church House Publishing, 2003.

4 Cf. Francis Bridger, 'A Theological Reflection' in *Guidelines for the Professional Conduct of the Clergy*, London: Church House Publishing, 2003, pp. 13–20.

5 Anthony Russell, *The Clerical Profession*, London: SPCK, 1980, p. 24.

6 Accessed online at http://www.newadvent.org/cathen/13694a.htm, 7 September 2007.

7 *Formation for Ministry*, 4.3–4.10 (37–40); the passage quoted is form 4.6 (38).

8 See notes 6 and 7 for references.

9 Samuel Amirtham and Robin Pryor (eds), *The Invitation to the Feast of Life: Resources for Spiritual Formation in Theological Education*, Geneva: World Council of Churches, 1989.

10 Cf. John Milbank, *The Suspended Middle: Henri de Lubac and the Debate Concerning the Supernatural*, London: SCM, 2005.

11 L. M. Rulla, F. Imoda and J. Ridick, *Psychological Structure and Vocation: A Study of the Motivations for Entering and Leaving the Religious Life*, Rome: Gregorian University Press, 1988.

12 Victor Turner, *The Ritual Process: Structure and Anti-structure*, Chicago: Aldine, 1969.

3

Gender, Spirituality and Power in Ministerial Formation

JUSTINE ALLAIN CHAPMAN

When leading Evening Prayer before class, our students recently have taken to directing the men to say the odd verses of the psalm and the women the even, rather than having the psalms said antiphonally from one side of the room to another. It took me a while to realize why my whole being seemed to recoil at this invitation to say psalms in this way, and I concluded that it has something to do with gender, spirituality and power. When I was training for ordination in the early 1990s, as a curate, as a vicar and as a member of deanery chapters, the even verses would have been said by me alone, or perhaps by one other, the odd verses by many more. The verses I would have said as an ordinand would have been said by those who couldn't be priests, as part of the gender that did not have institutional power. I say 'would have' because we didn't ever say psalms in this gendered way, since any female voices would have been drowned out. To say psalms in such a way now, in a student body that is a little over half women, means the volume is equal but it sounds different. It makes me ask whether women pray the words differently and whether some of the themes and aspirations of the psalm are voiced differently. In an academic staff team of eight where I am the only woman, I am conscious that not only do I look different since I do not conform to the jacket-and-tie dress code, but I sound different when we pray. I don't say the same verses of praise and prayer of the psalm as my colleagues – do I or do many of the female students we train pray, teach, preach and learn differently too?

I no longer recoil at the invitation to split by gender, now that I have identified how my history, as an ordinand and Anglican priest for as long as women have been priests, is playing its role. As I hear my voice among the voices of many other women, I rejoice that in the ministerial gatherings of tomorrow's churches the sound will have a balance and variety of voices and harmonies that were missing from such gatherings previously. It is tomorrow's churches for which we train students, but in the meantime, whether they be male or female, they will need to function in the institutional churches of today.

There has, of course, been a great deal of change for the Church and its training institutions since women's ordination. There has also been much that has not changed, but which needs to if theological education is to attend to the spiritual and ministerial education of those who will minister in the churches of today as well as have a role in the churches of tomorrow. In both the Church of England and the British Methodist Church, women ministers make up over one-third of the ministry. That's a considerable shift in the make-up of the clergy, but the numerical shift in terms of gender has not been matched with a shift in the balance of institutional power. Institutional power is largely held by a male clerical elite.[1] It is understandable therefore that one of the issues that the Church is currently looking to address is why there are so few women priests in senior positions. There is, of course, much critique of appointments procedures in addressing this, but there are also some disturbing indications that women are declining invitations to senior positions or are not applying for them. It seems that women are assessing whether the culture of working in the Church has become too difficult for them.

The authors of *Talent and Calling*, a recent report from the Church of England, state that they 'understand that one of the reasons why women are not appointed to senior positions is that the position is advertised but there is a reluctance of women to apply – either because of a belief that their gifts are not valued by the Church, or because the duties attached to the posts in question do not appeal to them'.[2] A number of issues emerged which were perceived to be possible barriers to women seeking senior appointment. Some of these were system and process issues for the Church, and others were issues that women clergy may wish to think about.[3] The findings of the report largely echo those of the Committee for Gender Justice of the British Methodist Church, which went so far as to conclude that: 'The British Methodist Church in Great Britain is suffering from institutional sexism.' It defined the term as follows:

Institutional sexism: The collective failure of an organization to provide appropriate services and opportunities to people because of their gender.[4]

The issue of the 'stained-glass ceiling' for women ministers is one that those in ministerial formation must address at the stage of training. What is it about the culture of the Church that is preventing women from hearing or responding to the call to fill senior posts that is reflected and even promoted in our training institutions?

At a local level, many congregations have now experienced women's ministry. Expectations about the change in culture that women clergy would bring to the Church at large have, however, not been fulfilled, and the hope that women would grow in their ministry and so take on more senior positions in the Church is not being realized as smoothly as many thought it would.

Ian Jones, in his study *Women and Priesthood in the Church of England Ten Years On*, used case studies, in-depth interviews and questionnaires to consider the experience of women priests in the Church of England. He discovered that there was some acknowledgement that the changes brought about by women's priesting did not yet seem to be 'as revolutionary as some had hoped, and others had feared.'[5] He found that participants in the study, clerical and lay, reported that women have brought additional gifts and insights through their priestly ministry and they also brought an expectation that women's priestly ministry would look different from men's priestly ministry. A majority, however, were reluctant to generalize too far about the respective qualities and attributes of men and women.[6] This echoes, he comments, the expectations of the changes that women priests would bring to the Church voiced around the time of the debate about ordaining women to the priesthood of the Church of England. Supporters of the ordination of women looked forward to benefits for the Church, Jones says, for 'at the most fundamental level, women's priesting would signal a shift away from a patriarchal Church, a theological injustice would be righted and the Church would be returned closer to the biblical vision of the Kingdom of God in which there was "neither Jew nor Greek, slave nor free, male or female"'.[7] For some, Jones describes how the promise of a new style of priesthood would come because of the experiences, perspectives and characteristics that women would bring as women, ushering in the demise of the 'old boys' network' and a relational and collaborative way of working.[8]

The title of Susan's Durber's book, *Preaching Like a Woman*, echoes Nicola Slee's book *Praying Like a Woman*. Twenty years ago there was much discussion as to how female ministers would or should be different from their male counterparts, as well as what that would mean for the Church and for the gospel. Now there is material that explores what some of those differences might be by observing and encouraging women and men to preach, pray and minister as themselves and to look at the gender dimension in that ministry.

These questions of the difference gender makes to the way in which ordained ministers conduct their ministry and how that is related to other dimensions of their lives as well as to the constraints and opportunities that the institutional Church provides are bigger than can be addressed here. However, there are several dimensions of formation which I will address in order to bring some insight regarding how we may best attend to the ministerial and spiritual formation of women as they prepare for public ministry. There has been recent work which has revealed differences about the faith development and spirituality of women. From other areas of life insights have come from the experiences of women in male-dominated businesses. The connecting thread between these is that women who work in institutions that have over time been shaped by men and masculine ways of doing things, very often feel under-confident and alienated and decide not to pursue or accept positions of responsibility. This is the situation that Churches which ordain women are seeking to address at the present time. It seems to be that encouraging and understanding patterns of spiritual growth and maturity experienced by women may go some way towards helping both the Church and those ordained to hear and respond to their calling. Spiritual growth, the shaping of a vocation and functioning in the world of work begin long before training for ordained ministry. Theological colleges and courses, however, are highly influential in furthering development in these areas. The vast majority of staff in these institutions are male and most often clergymen, who, since they have been working in such institutions and in parish ministry, will have most experience of working with other men as colleagues, rarely with women, and even more rarely with a woman as a superior. This means that particular attention needs to be given to the formation of women students to counteract the blind spots that homogenous groups carry. This is true also where the majority of a staff team are of one denomination, or are ordained. It is almost too obvious to say that more women need to be appointed in theological education and then to wonder why they are not responding to the job adverts or being appointed.

There are equal numbers of women and men in training, and for the foreseeable future they will be a minority among clergy. When clergy gather and dominate, especially on committees and boards, being part of a minority raises particular issues which if addressed can allow for all to make their contribution and be heard. It is not only, however, as ordained ministers that women will find themselves as the minority without institutional power. In training, both students male and female can experience being up against the masculine face of the institutional Church in ways they will not have experienced before and may well not experience again. The majority of our female students will find that on becoming an ordinand they encounter an entire hierarchy of male clergy under whose authority they now fall. They are most likely to have a male vicar or circuit colleague, male area dean or superintendent minister, male probationer secretary or diocesan director of ordinands, male tutor and male principal as they train, and then the chair or bishop at the top. If these women and the clergymen with whom they have dealings are unaware of some of the differences that gender may make to their formation, then their ministerial training may be less than it could be in supporting their spirituality and their ability to contribute effectively once ordained. When a female ordinand experiences being bullied by her superintendent, for example, the power and gender dynamics are such that it is difficult to speak out.

To give attention to the experiences of women could, of course, be interpreted as an implication that all women, and indeed all men, are the same. There will be some who wish to go quite a way down that road, some who would deny that there are gender differences and some who are tired with gender discussion and do not want to draw attention to them anymore. It is worth bearing in mind Leslie Francis' and David Musson's research on the personality types of clergy: 'male and female clergy tended to be somewhat atypical of their sexes; the usual contrasts between males and females do not hold among the clergy'. They found female ministers 'less outgoing, more assertive, less apprehensive, more socially controlled and less tense' than male ministers.[9] I have no intention of suggesting that all women think, feel, act, or pray in a certain way, or that they should. It seems to me that some of the experiences that shape women are to do with their social location and experience of being powerful or powerless in public and domestic life. That many ordained women find the structures of the institutional Church confining and overbearing, or clergy meetings dry and competitive, is not to say, of course, that many ordained men do not. It may well be that seeking to allow female voices to be heard and their experiences named may release what is less acknowledged in the experiences of men, and indeed of other groups of people whose testimonies will enrich our faith and renew our churches.

Women's faith development

There has been shock and discussion about the faith of Mother Teresa since the publication of private letters that she had requested be destroyed.[10] The letters reveal that for the last 50 years of her life she felt no presence of God whatsoever. In more than 40 letters she speaks of the 'dryness', 'darkness', loneliness', and the 'torture', that she is undergoing. She compares the experience to hell and at one point says that it has driven her to doubt the existence of heaven and of God. The revelations, though over an extraordinary length of time, are not surprising to those steeped in the spiritual classics, nor to mature spiritual directors. They are also of no surprise to those who know of the ordinary patterns and processes of women's faith development.

Training students for ordained ministry involves attention to issues of spiritual and ministerial formation in teaching, tutorials and community life, as well as requiring assessment of it when it comes to writing reports to sponsoring churches. In order even to attempt to assess spirituality over time it is important, in the first place, that we can understand how spiritual development for women might be different from that of men. This understanding should then support us in working towards creating the conditions for spiritual growth in our common life for women, for enabling all students to minister to women as well as helping us in the task of assessing both of these.

Research into the spiritual development of women is new. Nicola Slee comments, 'It is too soon to expect a fully elaborated model or theory of women's faith to emerge. At this point there are a number of rudimentary models of women's faith which can critique and expose the limitations of existing androcentric theories.'[11] The theory of faith development which Slee engages with and which is the one taught in most training institutions is that of James Fowler.[12] Slee does not discard Fowler's six-stage faith development theory out of hand, but argues that it neglects aspects of women's faith and needs to be corrected and broadened. In general, feminist critique of Fowler is directed, in the first place, towards his assertion that developmental change is consistent and unchanging across diverse cultural contexts. It then focuses on his placing of increased separation and autonomy as a more mature stage of faith than relationality. Fowler, like Erik Erikson, in his human development theory, has an implicit bias towards separation and autonomy as primary development goals which 'may describe typically male patterns of development in the Western world but do not do justice to women's experience of connectedness and relationality'.[13] Fowler's heroes, it is often noted, for example Dietrich Bonhoeffer and Jesus of Nazareth, are placed in Stage 6 and have moved beyond or given up intimate relationships or responsibility for dependents. These 'saints' are dead before their time, and exemplify a selfhood achieved at the expense of community, including their relationships with women.

Slee's doctoral research goes further than a critique of Fowler's theory in identifying three patterns of women's faith development. The generative themes she identifies as revealing core patterns in women's faith development are alienation, awakenings and relationality. They provide insight into what many women training for ministry may have experience of, and if not understood and named publicly, leave those women impoverished.

The theme of *alienation* in women's faith development that Slee identifies is characterized by 'women's experience of alienation, a profound loss of self, of authentic connection with others, and of faith'.[14] This alienation might be something the women have passed through or struggle with, and in a sense it represents a lack of development, for it is precisely a lack of movement, an impasse. Slee draws attention to others who have addressed this alienation. Carol Christ, who charted the loss of self and connection as a prevalent theme in contemporary women's fiction, describes it as

> an experience of nothingness, an emptiness, a self-hatred or self-negation which manifests itself in feelings of inadequacy, anxiety or disease, amnesia and loss of feeling, an inability to act, a sense of being imprisoned or trapped, a lack of meaning and sense of self, a vicarious living of the self through some other person or project (often a male partner) and a giving away of the self to be absorbed by the other.[15]

The experience of alienation is diverse but pervasive in women's spirituality, Slee asserts, and represents a major developmental challenge for women in a patriarchal culture. Slee discusses alienation as being related to the lack of roles available to women in mainstream patriarchal culture, and as being more profound in women who are socially deprived. It is also related to the difficulty many women have in answering the question, 'Who am I?'

Women describing the experience of alienation and paralysis do so with extraordinary creativity, using metaphors of wilderness and desert, confinement and enclosure, deadness, loss of feeling and reality, not knowing the self, disconnection, fragmentation, division, alienation, breakdown, paralysis and impasse, the quest or search for what is unknown, abdication, absorption or reckless giving up of the self to the (male) other as well as domination, oppression, violent attack or rape of the self. In the section on abdication, absorption or reckless giving up of the self to the 'male' other, Slee describes many of the women experiencing a

> loss of selfhood and authentic spirituality which was bound up with unauthentic relation to the other, and very often this other was the male

other – father, partner, lover or God. For these women, the loss of self was a result of, or another side of, the experience of giving oneself away to, being absorbed in, becoming excessively identified with and dependent upon the male other.[16]

Their struggle for authentic selfhood, Slee comments, was a struggle to find authentic ways of relating to the male in which the self is not threatened or overpowered. Where a woman's relationship with God

was modelled on dysfunctional or collusive relationships with men (particularly the father), there was a struggle to transform the relationship to the male God such that it no longer legitimated patterns of female passivity, abdication of selfhood or victimisation. For some women, this entailed a radical rejection of male God imagery, for others, a fundamental reworking of such imagery.[17]

The section on domination, oppression, violent attack or rape of the self describes the other side of inauthentic relationship to the male, where, rather than voluntarily giving away the self to the other, the self is experienced as being coerced, compelled, taken against its will and in the process, damaged, violated and abused. In relating to God, where this is internalized, 'the damage wreaked on the female psyche is profound, since male violence against the female becomes legitimised theologically and takes on the power of divine sanction'.[18]

Even for women who have not experienced overt physical or sexual abuse, the effects of living in a culture in which male violence is endemic are evident in women's descriptions of domination in its many different forms, both individual and instituitionalised.[19]

Women in Slee's study, in speaking of abdicating the self or becoming absorbed into the other, recognized by their use of such language the need to reclaim the self they had abandoned and exercise a rightful care of self. In her chapter on *awakenings*, Slee states that the

developmental challenge posed by the experience of impasse may lead, for women, to the liberating experience of awakening, breakthrough and reconnection to their own power of selfhood as well as to a deeper awareness of their connectedness to others and to the divine. Nevertheless this is neither automatic nor pain-free.[20]

Breakthrough or awakening to a new consciousness and spiritual vitality is described by a number of writers as a key component of women's spirituality. Carol Christ, in identifying awakening as a frequently used metaphor for mystics, suggests that it has particular characteristics for women. Whereas for men, conversion often entails the giving up of worldly power, for women 'awakening is not so much a giving up as a gaining of worldly power . . . Women often describe their awakening as a coming to self, rather than a giving up of self, as a grounding of selfhood in the powers of being, rather than a surrender of self to the powers of being'.[21] Other writers comment, in addition to the reclaiming of self, on themes of affirmation of the body and the importance of nature and female friendship.

Slee describes a variety of narratives of awakening, identifying themes of leaving home, making the break, separation; travel to another country, place or people; coming home, finding one's centre, coming to rest; the experience of motherhood; relating to the vulnerable, marginal or suffering other; discovering one's own creative voice or sphere; illness, suffering, death and other 'limit' situations. Slee identifies six common and defining features of awakening in women's spirituality:

- An emphasis on concrete, ordinary and mundane experience as the locus of spiritual awakening.
- The priority of intuition, bodily knowing and instinct over rational thinking, abstract thought of the dictates of conscience or authority; a period of preparation leading to breakthrough.
- A sense of coming together and coherence of different parts of the self acting in unity.
- Bringing together the sense of actively taking responsibility for the self with the sense of a process of unfolding or bringing to birth which goes far beyond conscious choice or control.
- A new naming of self, reality and God with the developmental challenge of reconstructing old models of selfhood as well as the received models from religion and spirituality.[22]

Slee's third major generative theme in women's spiritual development is that of *relationality*, a theme 'which has been dominant in many studies of women's spirituality and identity'.[23] Discriminating between different types of relationality in the recognition that not all relationship is good, is, of course, important.

Mary Grey, in discussing redemption, atonement and revelation in terms of relationality, sees two fundamental movements or poles to the process of redemption or reconnecting: self-affirmation on the one hand, and right relation on the other. Women in particular, she says, need to come to a sense of self before they can establish relation with others. The second pole of right relation is not so much in opposition to the process of self-affirmation as the context in which it occurs.[24] Metaphors that the women in Slee's research used to describe the 'relationship of the believer with God included hierarchical relational terms such as parent, sovereign or lord, but more frequently in relationships of mutuality as lover, partner or friend; and in both male and female imagery'.[25]

For some of the black women in the study there was less of an emphasis upon the interconnectedness of relationship with God and relationship with others, and a 'strong sense of the relationship with God as the source of oppositional power, sustaining the self in opposition to the forces of racism and oppression which they experienced in society and in the church, and which soured and skewed human relationships'.[26] One of the most powerful ways in which the women expressed a relational faith was through their profound empathetic connection to others in pain, involving a kind of self-emptying and an openness to vulnerability and change in the light of others' needs. The danger of such caring, if it does not include mutuality and the ability to challenge the other, is that it reinforces women's tendency to give the self away in an over-identification with the needs of the other.[27] Slee comments that a central struggle in the faith development of the women in her study was how to hold together the needs of the self and the demands of the other, intensified in the struggle to respond to the other's suffering without putting the self in jeopardy.[28] Women's capacity to bear the suffering of others without being overwhelmed by the enormity of pain seemed to depend on a variety of factors which were: the stability of their own sense of selfhood, rooted in a strong measure of self-acceptance and self-knowledge; their ability to receive from others, as well as care for them; their conviction in the redemptive presence of God in all human suffering; and their capacity to appropriate creatively their own pain and that of others in meaningful work, for example prayer, painting, preaching or pastoral ministry.[29] In contrast to Fowler's developmental descriptions, the women's accounts in Slee's study suggest 'the achievement of a more flexible and grounded self-in-relation via embeddedness in the demands of relationship rather than via separation and autonomy'.[30]

Implications

Slee's research indicates that there are distinctive patterns and processes in women's faith development. Not all women in all places will describe their faith in the ways that the women in her research did, and quite possibly there will be men whose experience of faith resonates with what she discovered. As a personal tutor of ministerial students, Slee's research has made sense of much of what I heard from women exploring their faith and calling. Just as the even-numbered verses of praise and prayer sound different from the odd verses, so do those voices as they speak of their faith; and gender as well as power has no little part to play.

It is perhaps the theme of alienation which is most surprising or difficult to address in ministerial formation. I have been made to wonder whether some diagnoses of depression may have more to do with the experience of alienation, an experience which is part of spiritual maturation. There does seem to be a tacit understanding that Christians, and particularly ordained ministers, need to speak about their faith in a way that is confident, articulate and certain. It can be very difficult to name doubt or confusion, to find oneself unable to bring forth coherent explanation in a tutorial or assignment. The themes raised under Slee's description of alienation are not named publicly, in worship or in class, except for the mystics. If the student's impasse is not acknowledged to be part of the pattern of faith, an unnecessary questioning of vocation and a loss of confidence can take place. Those who struggle with paralysis are left with a sense of not being good enough, of failure – and such invisibility inhibits their spiritual development as well as their effectiveness as pastors.

The strong experiential and relational bias in women's spirituality comes as no surprise to those familiar with feminist theological and educational discourse. Experiences of awakening were often triggered by common experiences such as travel, motherhood, relationships and artistic activity. In a climate where the heights of faith are presented as fleeing the mundane, denying the body and passions and putting religious ideals over the demands of connection faith grounded in experience can seem second class and unacademic. Belenky and her co-writers have advocated educational methods which begin with women's personal experience, are strongly contextual and geared towards a pragmatic, lived knowledge which relates theoretical and abstract understanding to the demands of real women's lives. From the point of view of the teacher, this is demanding, not least because it takes a great deal of time to present material in very different ways from the ones in which you were taught. It is, however, what has been expected in school teaching and increasingly in higher education for some time. The educational and pastoral practices of the Church seem not to engage at times with common practice elsewhere, though this is less so at local level.

Each theological institution will have to decide upon the spiritual climate that underlies what it does. It may not be that there is the intention, in teaching or in worship, to place ordinary and personal experience in second place; but a celebration of the lives of the saints and a course in church history by implication might well honour the martyr and the monk, and say little of faith in the everyday. There is a strong emphasis on experience acknowledged in women's liturgy as well as in women's preaching, as both Elaine Graham and Susan Durber show. Kathleen Fischer points to the importance of experience in the spiritual direction of women, as is also clear from a glance at the programmes of retreat houses. Retreats for ordinands and ordination retreats may well, however, take a more traditional and masculine form for the most part. For some theological institutions, it may be worth reflection whether the early morning and evening times of prayer honour the call to parenthood and to relationships that are being upheld elsewhere.

There are enough female students in theological education for there to be occasions for female-only groups, which may provide women with opportunities for sharing and exploring. Women-only groups have a long history in churches, of course, but are rare in theological education. I am conscious that the lack of this opportunity for female-only groups when the first generation of women priests was in training is a difficulty which has legacies for relationships between women clergy now.

That women mature in faith in the context of reconnecting and gaining right relationship with others causes me to question whether common emphases in worship and Christian speech more generally, on self-emptying, surrender and submission as aspirations of spiritual maturity, are ones that can guide women students in particular in spiritual growth and then sustain them in ministry. Most of our students are women who are giving much to their families and the Church in work which is neither time-bound nor paid. Slee's research, supported by much feminist theology, indicates that it is gaining a sense of self that many women struggle with, something related to self-esteem and self-confidence.

Women in public ministry

Affirming, encouraging and assessing spiritual formation is part of the task of the theological educator. Preparing students for public ministry in today's Church is another. Where the gender balance of students is equal, both male and female students are less prepared for the imbalance they will experience when part of the clergy. Helping students to recognize and deal with some of the gender and power dynamics at work will assist in helping to realize the hopes of many who pray for a Church that is itself a herald of the kingdom. This will in turn stem the flow of ordained women, who, in turning down senior posts, indicate that the culture of the institutional Church is not yet whole and does not enable all to speak and be heard.

That there are few women in senior positions and that women may well be declining invitations to senior positions comes as no surprise to Peninah Thomson and Jacey Graham, who, in their qualitative study *A Woman's Place is in the Boardroom*, with Tom Lloyd have studied the 'marzipan layer', that is the management layer just below the board. This book was the one set as recommended reading at the consultation in October 2006 set up by Archbishops' Secretary for Appointments to look at what might be done to encourage appointment of women to senior positions. Their research has much that is transferable to the Church of England, or indeed other denominations.

In their chapter 'Priming the Pipeline' (in their context the pipeline is the number of women who could be candidates for board appointments in the foreseeable future), Thomson and Graham identify several features which make it difficult for women to contribute effectively in their work setting. These include feeling alone and losing confidence. Experiencing easy and warm relationships becomes more difficult and complex, as 'minor actions and remarks acquire significance in the rarefied atmosphere. Personal strategies and tactics that worked well enough previously seem less effective.'[31] The research indicates that some women come to senior jobs feeling that they don't belong there. Part of the reasons for this is that many women 'may prefer informal structures and relationships, but when moving up to a senior role, they are entering a level where structures and relationships may be a good deal more formal. They must learn to live with that. And although they may loathe office politics, they must recognise that they now work at a level where politics are endemic and unavoidable.'[32]

How it is most desirable that the culture of the Church should change cannot be our remit here, but that the women in training for ordained ministry are enabled, empowered and equipped to exercise that ministry is something that the institutions that train them can begin to address. Thomson and Graham argue that 'to achieve the long-term cultural changes needed to bring more women up to board level, change is required in three areas: individual, team and systems'.[33] In training, it is the individual on whom there is most focus. Gender balance of the student body provides, at least, the opportunities for future clergy team working to be more effective, and the internal systems of theological institutions can no doubt improve with regard to gender. That clergy generally work on their own, running their own show or with one other priest, means that it is possible to avoid the institution of the Church to a large extent and get on with one's ministry.

The shift from being a lay member of a ministry team to being an ordinand and then ordained can be experienced in similar ways to the move to the board position with increased formality and politics, described by Thomson and Graham. In addition, a lack of confidence is also common. Anne Dickson notes in *Women at Work: Strategies for Survival and Success* that 'women who are either middle or senior managers do not operate from a core of high self-esteem: privately they often feel lonely, unconfident and are working excessively hard to compensate for self-perceived inadequacy'.[34] She comments that 'on one hand is the high level of academic or professional qualification and experience of these women, their intelligence, their talents, their commitment and dedication; while on the other is a vivid picture of internal doubts, misgivings and anxieties stemming from an abiding, and sometimes disabling, lack of confidence'.[35]

It is this lack of confidence which draws me to ask what theological and spiritual resources can be offered to those in training to help them contribute effectively as public ministers and to recognize the importance of doing so. With regard to practical strategies, Dickson's book seeks to provide 'practical skills and suggestions as to how to develop a genuine belief in your own ability to communicate, to be effective, to manage your authority and weather the storms of working life with more confidence'.[36] Her particular approach is derived from the work of American behavioural psychologists and emphasizes responsible expression of emotion, the relevance of assertive skills to sexuality and a commitment to equality.[37] The approach that institutions which train public ministers might develop is one that not only affirms and allows for a diversity of rhythm and melody in the spiritual and ministerial experience of the students, but by attention to the differences that gender can make to formation, prepares ministers to enable all God's people to voice the good news that their faith proclaims in their lives.

Conclusion

There has been much that has changed in theological education that takes account of the perspectives and preferences of women in recent years. Feminist theology is now taught as mainstream. In relation to Scripture, working positively with stories of biblical women, remembering and mourning women's pain in 'texts of terror', listening to silences and employing imagination are all much more common than they were 20 years ago. Teaching methods, including the setting of assignments, in many educational establishments have been influenced by feminist discourse and research into adult education, and place a stronger focus on grounding learning in experience and teaching using the creative arts. These benefit many students, from a variety of backgrounds. Being taught in creative ways, of course, enables students to go on to teach in ways that are more accessible to more people in our churches. There is more that can improve in this direction. One area relates to appointments. Institutions that train ministers need to be attentive to the teaching experience and style of theological educators when making appointments. Such appointments can fall unhelpfully between the need for a proven academic record, in order to satisfy the higher education provider, and the needs of those training for ministry. This can be the case not only in relation to methods of teaching, but also in the suitability of an applicant to be a personal tutor charged with accompanying and assessing spiritual and ministerial formation.

Any exploration of the influence of gender in our churches is felt at a gut level, by men and by women, because our gender is very close to our personal identity. It is tempting to brush discussion about gender, spirituality and power to one side, perhaps because we think enough has been done for the time being and we hope that change will happen naturally as more women come through the system. Alternatively, we might brush such discussion under the carpet for fear of the anger that can be expressed and the hurt reopened, particularly when discussions at the level of staff and committee meetings will not be conducted in teams where there is gender balance or an equal holding of power between the genders.

In this chapter, I have attempted to attend to some patterns of spirituality, preferences in learning and experiences of women in public ministry which may enable those of us who seek to assist the spiritual and ministerial formation of women and men to look at what we do and who we are. We need to be prepared to change, adjust and name in our teaching, preaching and one-to-one encounters experiences of Christian women that are invisible or in the background, in order that they, and others, may be better helped to find freedom in Christ and in Christ's Church.

That the majority of those who have the power to effect change are men can mean that something akin to colonial guilt can set in. This may be inevitable, but in the meantime I want to alert ordained women, women ordinands and women theological educators to what we may do to proclaim the faith in ways which best resonate with the people that we are, including our gender. One of the disturbing results of the research regarding women in the workplace is the designation of some women as Queen Bees. Queen Bees are women who like being the sole representative of their gender at the top of their organizations. This gives them cachet among their male colleagues, which would be diluted along with the arrival of more women, and so it is in their interests to do nothing and pull the ladder up behind them. Some women do not deliberately make it harder for other women, but having got to the top feel under no obligation to make the climb easier for women. Thomson and Graham comment that 'senior women speak with great authority on gender issues. If they tell their male colleagues that nothing needs to be done, who can gainsay them?'[38] This Queen Bee syndrome, when added to Thomson and Graham's observation that it is with other women that women are most competitive, echoes the ambivalent comments of women priests in Jones' survey when discussing networks of women priests and the role of bishops' advisors for women. As women we must ask ourselves whether we are complicit in preventing other women from flourishing in faith and ministry by the things we do not say or do, as well as by the ways we interact with colleagues.

The identification of lack of confidence and a reluctance to put oneself forward is well known among groups of clergywomen, and there has been, for a long time, a call to women to encourage other women to take up roles and apply for jobs. Meeting together in groups as women clergy for support is patchy, and there can be a generational divide between those who bear battle scars from before the ordination of women to the priesthood and those who have been selected and trained since then. For some, there is the temptation to urge that, having got this far, we mustn't rock the boat any more; for some, there is a temptation to sink into simmering resentment about the ways things are. That more women speak out about their experience of faith and ministry and speak honestly of the delights, small irritations as well as real difficulties, will mean that there can be more discussions that recognize and value that women are not all the same, but may experience broadly similar difficulties which, if addressed, can benefit the whole Church, clergy and lay. Locating the struggles of one's experience in order to seek healing, to identify them and use them to accompany others on the journey of faith, and finding an appropriate way to voice where there is injustice, is part of any Christian's call. It is something that women in, and training for, ministry must be attentive to for the sake of the whole body of Christ today, and for its daughters and sons of tomorrow.

Gender statistics

Church of England

The 2007 Church of England report *Talent and Calling*, in addressing the proportion of women among the various ranks of the clergy, states that 'by 2005 the majority (52%) of ordained local ministers and almost half (46%) of non-stipendiary ministers were women; women made up 36% of the diocesan clergy overall . . . In 2005 20% of full-time stipendiary clergy and 23% of clergy of incumbent status (though only 9% of incumbents) were women.'[39]

Remembering that there are no women bishops, the other senior positions that women can occupy are in cathedrals and as archdeacons. Currently in the Church of England there are '43 deans, 120 archdeacons and 140 residentiary canons'.[40] The report states that 'in January 2007 there were eleven female archdeacons (10.2%), of whom three had not yet taken up their posts, two female deans (5.0%) and 17 female residentiary canons (13.9%)'.[41] There are, then, no women bishops and 30 women out of 303 possible positions at what is considered to be the next level.

British Methodist Church

The Gender Justice monitoring report of 2003/2004 reported that the number of female presbyters in active work was 35% of the total. While this was a slight increase, the increase needed to be set against the fact that out of 607 superintendents, only 85 were female. More distressing was the fact that the ratio of women without an appointment to that of men without an appointment is 2:1. The report asked:

> Are there bars to women becoming ministers in Methodism? The argument of no-go areas is still as valid as three years ago; evidence from the findings shows that 58% of our Methodist Districts have less than 30% female presbyters stationed out of their total active stations. One

District has less than 10% female presbyters of its total and one other District has no female presbyters at all. Is this gender equality?[42]

With regard to Connexional ministry and representation on Church committees, the figures were similarly disconcerting: there was no ordained woman serving on the Connexional team, there were only two female Chairs of District, and both roles were as co-chair. Of the 29 connexional committees examined, only one has more women than men, nine are without an ordained female as opposed to only two without an ordained male. The conclusion reached was that 'the picture only worsens. Women are represented less than before in our committees Connexionally.'[43]

Notes

1 See pp. 71–2 for statistical information on women in ministry in the Church of England and the British Methodist Church.

2 The Archbishops' Council, *Talent and Calling: A Review of the Law and Practice Regarding Appointments to the Offices of Suffragan Bishop, Dean, Archdeacon and Residentiary Canon*, GS 1650, London: General Synod of the Church of England, 4.2.11, 2007, p. 36.

3 *Talent and Calling*, 4.2.12, p. 36.

4 The British Methodist Church, *Methodist Church Committee for Gender Justice: Methodist Conference 2002 Report*, Peterborough: The British Methodist Church, 2001.

5 Ian Jones, *Women and Priesthood in the Church of England Ten Years On*, London: Church House Publishing, 2004, p. 205.

6 Jones, *Women and Priesthood*, pp. xi–xii.

7 Jones, *Women and Priesthood*, p. 82.

8 Jones, *Women and Priesthood*, p. 82.

9 L. Francis and D. Musson, 'Male and Female Anglican Clergy: Gender Reversal on the 16PF?', *Journal of Empirical Theory*, 12, 1999, pp. 5–16, cited in Fraser Watts, Rebecca Nye and Sarah Savage, *Psychology for Christian Ministry*, London: Routledge, 2002, p. 251.

10 Brian Kolodiejchuk and Mother Teresa, *Come Be My Light: The Private Writings of the Saint of Calcutta*, New York: Doubleday, 2007. See also David Van Biema, 'Mother Teresa's Critics of Faith' in *Time*, 23 August 2007.

11 Nicola Slee, *Women's Faith Development: Patterns and Processes*, Aldershot: Ashgate, p. 168.

12 See James Fowler, *Stages of Faith: The Psychology of Human Development and the Quest for Meaning*, San Francisco: Harper & Row, 1981, or a summary in Slee, *Women's Faith Development*, pp. 29–32.

13 Slee, *Women's Faith Development*, p.18.

14 Slee, *Women's Faith Development*, p. 81.

15 Carol Christ, *Diving Deep and Surfacing: Women Writers on Spiritual Quest*, Boston: Beacon Press, 1986, cited in Slee, *Women's Faith Development*, p. 82.

16 Slee, *Women's Faith Development*, pp. 100, 101.

17 Slee, *Women's Faith Development*, p. 101.

18 Slee, *Women's Faith Development*, p. 104.

19 Slee, *Women's Faith Development*, p. 105.

20 Slee, *Women's Faith Development*, p. 109.

21 Christ, *Diving Deep and Surfacing*, p. 19, cited in Slee, *Women's Faith Development*, p. 110.

22 Slee, *Women's Faith Developmen*, p. 133, 134.

23 Slee, *Women's Faith Development*, p. 135.

24 Mary Grey, *The Wisdom of Fools: Seeking Revelation for Today*, London: SPCK, 1986, cited in Slee, *Women's Faith Development*, p. 137.

25 Slee, *Women's Faith Development*, p. 140.

26 Slee, *Women's Faith Development*, p. 145.

27 C.L. Hess, *Caretakers of our Common House: Women's Development in Communities of Faith*, Nashville, Abingdon, 1997, p. 96ff, cited in Slee, *Women's Faith Development*, p. 149.

28 Slee, *Women's Faith Development*, p. 149.

29 Slee, *Women's Faith Development*, p. 151.

30 Slee, *Women's Faith Development*, p. 159.

31 P. Thomson and J. Graham with T. Lloyd, *A Woman's Place is in the Boardroom*, London: Palgrave Macmillan, 2005, p. 164.

32 Thomson and Graham, *A Woman's Place*, p. 167.

33 Thomson and Graham, *A Woman's Place*, p. 189.

34 Anne Dickson, *Women at Work: Strategies for Survival and Success*, London: Kogan Page, 2000, p. 9.

35 Dickson, *Women at Work*, p. 1.

36 Dickson, *Women at Work*, p. 1.

37 Dickson, *Women at Work*, p. 7.

38 Thomson and Graham, *A Woman's Place*, p. 164.

39 *Talent and Calling*, 4.2.1, p. 34.

40 *Talent and Calling*, 4.5.5, p. 40.

41 *Talent and Calling*, 4.2.2. p. 34.

42 The Methodist Church of Great Britain, *The Next Step: Continuing our Commitment to the Ministry of the Whole People of God*, 2003, p. 5.

43 *The Next Step*, p. 6.

4

Made for Ordination

ANGELA SHIER-JONES

You did not choose me but I chose you. And I appointed you to go and bear fruit, fruit that will last, so that the Father will give you whatever you ask him in my name. (John 15.16)

Introduction

To what extent are ministers made by the Church through the processes of selection and training, or ordained by God to the work of the kingdom? This is not a rhetorical question, but one that defines the power and authority of the ordained ministry of the Church. If ministers are primarily made, then their power derives from those who make them and shape them, and their authority is largely institutional, acquired by virtue of the office that they bear. If, on the other hand, ministers are ordained, then their power resides in the sacramental synergism of God and Church in faith and order, grace and charism, and their authority is a derivative of the authority of the gospel. Given the fallen and incomplete nature of the Church and the inability of humanity to be fully obedient to the will of God, the answer to the question undoubtedly lies somewhere in between these two extremes. Ministers are both made and ordained, with power and authority derived from both the Church and from God; for the Church is not in opposition to God, but rather seeks, institutionally, to act in accordance with what it believes is God's will with regard to the making of ministry.

Many ministers would describe their Service of Ordination as a pivotal moment in their life. It is a holy and defining moment of testing who they are before God and before the people, when it is at once testified to, affirmed, and made possible. Every attempt is made to enable those who share in such a service to be aware that they are participating in an act of profound significance which publicly and permanently changes the lives of all those concerned, not just the ordinand him- or herself. For some, the service follows three or more years of preparation and training; for others, it is the culmination of a longer process of discernment, training and formation which includes two or more years of ministerial practice. For all ordinands, it is a moment of transition and transformation.

Yet, in spite of its clear significance to both the Church and the ordinand, the role of ordination as a dimension of ministerial formation is seldom discussed. This may be due in part to the very different theologies of ordination held by the main denominations, and the shared desire, for the sake of greater ecumenicity, to avoid known areas of conflict. Another reason perhaps might be the difficulty in fitting the work of grace that ordination signifies into a table of practical outcomes for ministerial formation, to say nothing of finding some means of assessing it. The Church has a history of so predetermining what it is that makes a good minister a good minister that the potential for ordination to operate as a divinely appointed means of grace has been actively denied to some people. Yet Scripture and history both bear witness to the astonishing power of grace to transform the most unlikely candidates into ministers of the gospel as the need arises. It is this testimony, coupled with the conviction that we are living in a time of tremendous opportunity for mission, that makes the exploration of the real or potential contribution of ordination to ministerial formation so essential. This chapter will therefore seek to make explicit the opportunities for formation that are provoked by the tension between the making of ministry by the Church through its processes of selection, training and preparation for ordination, and the creation of ministry as a work of God's grace.

Made to order?

All ministry originates in the imperative to proclaim the good news of Jesus Christ and to ensure that the Church is built up in love. Far from being fixed and set in stone, the ministry of the Church has historically possessed an almost chameleon-like tendency to take on the appearance of the people it needs both to address and to attract in order that it might serve the present age. As Paul confessed:

> To the Jews I became as a Jew, in order to win Jews. To those under the law I became as one under the law (though I myself am not under the law) so that I might win those under the law. To those outside the law I became as one outside the law (though I am not free from God's law but am under Christ's law) so that I might win those outside the

law. To the weak I became weak, so that I might win the weak. I have become all things to all people, so that I might by any means save some. I do it all for the sake of the gospel, so that I may share in its blessings. (1 Corinthians 9. 20–23)

One of the best modern illustrations of this is the way in which the nature and perception of priesthood changed following the First World War in order to be able to address the changed population and recruit to parish ministry.

The Church of England's Convocation of 1900 had already taken note of the fact that ordinations to the diaconate were decreasing while the population of the country was increasing at a rate of 300,000 a year. This has been attributed to a variety of sources, but Stewart Mills noted that in particular: 'The success of the High Church movement with its clergy, cassocks and incense raised suspicions about the masculinity of clergy that in the age of Empire detracted from clerical vocations.'[1]

The decline in those offering for ministry from the more 'traditional sources' such as the universities and public schools had led to a desperate shortage of parish priests which was further exacerbated by the First World War. The vision that enabled the Church to resolve this crisis and recruit from alternative sources by overcoming the class distinction that was characteristic of its ministry prior to the war was inspired by Philip Clayton. Clayton had responded in 1915 to a request for more Army chaplains during the First World War. Unlike the other five chaplains serving in Ypres at that time taking parade services, conducting funerals and the like, Clayton succeeded in persuading the Senior Chaplain, Neville Talbot, to allow him to open a Church Army club. The club, named Talbot House after the brother of the Senior Chaplain who had been killed at Hooge, was run on civilian lines rather than according to military rules. This enabled it to become a neutral haven where rank was not important: 'Outside Clayton's room was the sign "Rank abandone ye who enter here". Another sign read: "If you are in the habit of spitting on the carpet, please spit here".'[2]

The primary purpose of Clayton's vision was to offer a pastoral ministry to the men of Flanders plain. Talbot House became a place of genuine respite. It was a home from home which allowed the soldiers, enlisted and officers alike, to lay aside their pain, grief, fear and dread for long enough to be renewed and restored. The chapel of Talbot House was called the 'Upper Room' by virtue of being housed in a converted garret, and it was here that Clayton celebrated the Eucharist and kept his infamous war roll. Unlike the traditional war roll recording the names of all those who had died, Clayton's roll was a list of all those who had pledged that if they survived the war, they would offer the rest of their lives to Christ in the service of the Church.

Mills narrates how the Archbishop of Canterbury recognized the potential of the men he saw at Talbot House when he visited in 1916 and where he undoubtedly read the roll. It was Talbot House that lay behind his historic pledge that 'no one suited for the ministry would be denied training due to financial hardship'.[3] This led eventually to the setting up of the General Fund to meet training costs and opened the way for enlisted men as well as officers to honour their pledge. As many as 675 men passed through the college that the Church created in response to Talbot's vision, 435 of whom were eventually ordained. It was a costly venture for the Church, but according to Mills it had two very important outcomes: first, it saved the parish system from collapse, and second, it effectively ended the class barrier to ministry in the Church of England.

To this could be added that the Church of England had effectively reshaped itself according to the particular mission and needs of the time. Intentional or not, this was highly providential. The new ministers were very different from their predecessors and, given their backgrounds, were unquestionably better placed to respond to the spiritual needs of a country that would all too soon find itself at war once again. Many of the ex-soldiers, like Bishop John Leonard Wilson, were clearly not your typical English gentleman pastor of yesteryear, 'but he as a prisoner of the Japanese in Changi Prison in the Second World War demonstrated what it was to be a true *pastor bonus*'.[4]

It is worth noting here that two complementary changes were necessary for the Church to make this ministry possible. First, the selection criteria needed to change to prevent the exclusion of a whole class of men on the grounds of academic ability and/or background alone. Second, ministerial training needed to change as it was no longer safe to presume (if indeed it ever was) that the ordinand had received the necessary education to fulfil the sacerdotal duties of a parish priest.

This chameleon-like ability of the Church to make ministry match people and vice versa has obvious advantages in mission but it also puts the Church at considerable risk of inadvertently but perhaps irrevocably reshaping all of ministry on the basis of a single specific 'focus' for mission. The awareness of this danger is found throughout the current reports dealing with those whom the Church of England is referring to as ordained pioneer ministers. It is evident elsewhere in responses to the recurrent question of whether or not evangelists should be ordained, and if so, to what order. The Baptist Union has formally recognized evangelists as accredited ministers, making it possible for ordinands to be received and ordained as either a pastor or an evangelist. Other denominations, including the British Methodist Church, have explored the necessity of providing specialized training for evangelists, culminating in an appropriate service of recognition and reception or commissioning. There is, however, general agreement among the denominations that while an evangelist may be ordained, it is not to an order of evangelists. As with the new ordained pioneer ministers of the Church of England, what is intended is ordination to 'a particular *focus* within the one ordained ministry of the church'.[5]

The difference is important as it demands that all those preparing for ordained pioneer ministry, or its equivalent in different denominations, undergo the same basic selection, training and formation processes as any other ordained minister of the Church. The nature of ministry clearly underwent a significant change at the start of the twentieth century as was evident by the changes it forced in the Churches' selection criteria and training. By safeguarding these twin processes, the Church expects to avoid such a significant change again, and to prevent the creation of a new order of ministry. The belief is that ministry should remain largely the same, even if the particular focus of mission alters during the lifetime of the minister. It remains to be seen how realistic an expectation this is.

The bishops' selection advisors are already asked to be aware that candidates for ordained pioneer ministry: 'will not necessarily see themselves as committed to more traditional expressions of ministry, though the calling to ordained ministry is lifelong and not to specific ministerial roles'.[6] Keeping pioneer ministry as a specific focus of existing orders of ministry will not be easy. The particular callings, commitments and charisms of pioneer ministry will need to be located among the charisms, callings and commitments already expected of those in more 'traditional' ordained ministry. Changes in the social or educational prerequisites for ordination can, on one level, be deemed to be quite superficial, compared to the sort of charismatic and character differences currently being wrestled with.

The language of 'missionary entrepreneurs', for example, seems strangely out of place alongside expressions such as 'servant ministry'. The extent to which personal charisms are emphasized in most writings on fresh expressions and emergent church ministry is difficult to reconcile with the conviction that all ministry is a sharing in the royal priesthood. As the Anglican theologian John Macquarrie notes, 'no man's personal qualities can sustain the weight of the ministry and the effectiveness of the office does not stand or fall with the man himself'.[7] It is not that shared ministry is denied in fresh expressions or pioneer ministries, it is simply that, in an age when the cult of the individual is celebrated, it is harder than ever to affirm and hold on to the unity and equality of the royal priesthood and the collegiality of the ordained ministry.

The Church has traditionally maintained this unity, equality and collegiality by acting as a gatekeeper to the ordained ministry. In ordination, states Macquarrie, 'those who have themselves the ministerial office and have been constituted the guardians of the Church's faith, test the calling of the ordinand and, if satisfied, admit him to office in the Church'. In his view, ordination is the outward form of the calling to a specific ministry in exactly the same way that baptism is the outward form of every Christian's call to be a part of the general ministry of Christ. Moreover, without ordination, 'the door is opened to chaos and the disintegration of the Church'.[8]

It is for this reason that, in addition to the outward expression or gifting of a calling to ministry, every minister must be trained and examined according to criteria which are not as easily altered for a specific context for mission. The selection criteria for pioneer ministers accordingly notes that it is not sufficient for candidates to have demonstrated their evangelistic or pioneering gifts, they must also be able to demonstrate that they recognize those same gifts as having been given for the benefit of the whole people of God under the oversight of the Church. Even Paul's pioneering ministry to the gentiles, in spite of his claim that it was commissioned directly by Christ, was still conducted under the auspices of the Church when, along with Barnabas, he was 'ordained' for it by the laying on of hands at the Church in Antioch (Acts 13.2–3).

Throughout the history of the Church, there have been other pioneering, charismatic leaders who were essential to its growth and mission. There have also been those who have, by force of their personal charisms, led to a fracturing of the unity of the Church. The Church has therefore learned the hard way to balance a healthy distrust of the 'personal' with an optimism of grace when considering candidates for the ordained ministry. Selection criteria and subsequent training still play a crucial role in defending the Church against the consequences that could follow from listening more to the spirit of the times than to the will of the Holy Spirit.

In recent church history, whenever the Churches have been pressured to change the training and selection criteria for ordination, they have responded with extreme caution and made changes only after considerable deliberation. This has caused a great deal of pain and frustration to those who believe that they have been called to ministry, and to those who believe that they are without the sort of minister that they need. The cry from those within the Catholic tradition who wrestle with their Church's insistence on a male celibate priesthood in spite of repeated calls for change is 'Sacrementa propter homines. Sacraments are there for the people.'[9] The Church's earlier pragmatism for the sake of the gospel lends credence to the validity of this cry. History teaches that mission makes its own practitioners and that the Church worldwide tends to grow from such practices – even if individual denominations tend to falter or decline. The Church that stifles the opportunities for mission by being too cautious over those it ordains can be accused of having lost sight of one of the primary purposes of ordination – namely, to teach and preach the good news.

It is helpful to set the contemporary restrictions on ordination alongside an earlier response to mission, namely the early church practice of ordaining male infants. As strange as this might seem, Michael Slusser has pointed out that not only was this done, but until relatively recently 'it has been the common opinion of Catholic theologians that the Church has the power to ordain male infants'.[10] The teaching of Pope Benedict XIV makes explicit reference to boy-deacons in the Coptic Church, and he is cited by others as an authority for the possibility of ordaining male infants before they were capable of reason. Noldin provides the rationale for the doctrine:

> A boy is validly ordained before he has the use of reason: for an infant is capable of those sacraments which do not demand a condition which he cannot fulfil, like matrimony, and which do not require the ability to sin, like penance and extreme unction, for orders does not require the recipient to do anything. But a boy ordained this way is given the choice, after he has sufficient use of reason, either of ministering in the order he has received or of passing over to worldly commitments; but when he has chosen he is thenceforth bound to fulfil the obligations of the order he has received and to persevere in it.[11]

Although the ordination was recognized as valid, it was also considered illicit, as Pope Benedict XIV had interpreted the Council of Trent in such a way that it not only stipulated the qualities that an individual needed to possess prior to ordination, but also the minimum ages. At that time it was taught that a person needed to be age 22 for the sub-diaconate, 23 for the diaconate, 25 for the presbyterate and 30 for the episcopate.[12] Thomas Aquinas, in arguing for the validity of the practice, however, simply notes that when those who were ordained as infants mature and begin to practise their ministry, it was not deemed necessary to repeat their ordination. The practice of ordaining infants probably had a practical liturgical root. The priest of a small Christian community may not have had anyone suitably ordained to assist them at certain liturgical celebrations. The obvious solution was to ordain a boy, perhaps their own son, to assist at the service.

This historic anomaly may seem absurd in the light of current debates about women's ordination and the ordination of married clergy, but it nonetheless alerts us to the potential role of ordination as a mediator of God's providential grace. The fact that the Church no longer ordains infants would imply that it no longer believes (if it ever did) in the efficacy of ordination alone in the making of ministers who can bear the fullness of ministry in their maturity.

Could the practice of ordaining infants, however, be an illustration of how someone is made a minister by virtue of their ordination? Being required to live up to the expectations of others can be a negative experience, but so also can not having any expectations at all to live up to: the one runs the risk of being too restrictive or oppressive, the other of being interpreted as a sign of indifference. The lack of younger candidates for the ordained ministry may be due in no small part to the lack of faith shown in them earlier on in their lives. The age limits and other external criteria set for ordination, however, may also be a contributing factor as they neither challenge young people to consider ordination, nor act to convince them of their potential for a 'higher calling'. The belief that John Wesley was a 'brand plucked from the burning' and that God had a 'divine' purpose for his life compelled his mother Susannah to take extra care over his 'formation' and undoubtedly impacted on Wesley's own conviction that he had a 'calling to fulfil'. Are we perhaps missing an opportunity to inspire, motivate and challenge young people by not ordaining in expectation? Would there be some value in a 'junior' order of presbyters and deacons?

The counter to such a proposal is that all Christians are ordained into a holy order: by virtue of their baptism, all Christians are part of the royal priesthood. The extent to which this is either recognized or promoted as a position of communal and ecclesial as well as personal responsibility, however, varies among the denominations. The practice of infant baptism creates a distance between the sacramental act of 'ordination' to this priesthood and the time when the responsibilities of the priestly office are taken up. Although confirmation and membership services serve to remind people of the dual nature of their discipleship, the increasing clericalization of the Church has undoubtedly lessened the awareness of the general 'priestly' responsibilities bestowed by the rite. Theologically, every denomination insists that the royal priesthood remains an important concept, but there is little evidence of this importance in practice.

Almost without exception, the Churches have voiced concerns over dwindling lay leadership and lay vocations. The day-to-day 'work' of the Church is predominantly clerically led, almost regardless of the nature of the work. Ordained ministers are just as likely to chair finance committees and have oversight of building projects as they are to chair pastoral committees and have oversight of mission projects.

To be ordained is to accept, under discipline, the implicit and explicit expectations of a particular order. The expectations with regard to both character and charism of those who are ordained is not limited to the specificities of the diaconate, presbyterate or episcopate but also varies with the ecclesial context in which the ministry is set. Someone ordained a deacon in the Church of England, for example, is ordained to a very different set of expectations from someone ordained to the diaconate in the British Methodist Church. Ordination is an act of the Church, of the gathered people of God, but, regardless of how theologically desirable it might be, it is first and foremost an act of a particular expression of church, not of the Church universal. This is in keeping with the First Council of Nicea in 325, which prohibited absolute ordinations to the 'universal Church' and limited the scope of ordination to the 'local' church in canons 15 and 16:

> Neither bishop, nor presbyter, nor deacon shall be transferred from city to city. But they shall be sent back should they attempt to do so, to the Churches in which they were ordained.
>
> Such presbyters or deacons as desert their own Church are not to be admitted into another, but are to be sent back to their own diocese. But if any bishop should ordain one who belongs to another Church without the consent of his own bishop, the ordination shall be cancelled.[13]

Although denominational boundaries have now largely replaced 'city' and/or diocesan boundaries, the spirit of these early canons is still respected by most Churches. This is evidenced by the different ordination and induction liturgies as well as by the lack of interchangeability of ministry from one Church to another and the language used to describe such little accommodation as can be made. For example, the Methodist Church has a process whereby ministers of other denominations can be 'recognized and regarded' as having a ministry equivalent to that of a Methodist presbyter or deacon.

Ordination is therefore first and foremost set in a denominational context which is generally non-transferable. This affects the formation of the ordinand who needs to be trained to be conversant with the particular contextual expectations of that denomination so that they can minister effectively within it. The failure of ecumenical ministerial training to fully address this dimension of formation has had long-term consequences for both the Methodist and the United Reformed Church traditions. Ecumenical training which does not adequately address denominational formation leads inevitably to the loss of the specific theological, spiritual and liturgical practices that release the ministerial charism of each denomination. This, as is now being realized, impoverishes the wider Church as well as the denominations, and endangers future ecumenism.

Perhaps one of the strongest reasons for supposing that ministers are predominantly made by the Church for parish or circuit ministry rather than ordained by God for the work of the kingdom is that not all denominations ordain to all three orders of ministry. The Methodist Church, for example, only ordains to the diaconate and the presbyterate.[14] There is, moreover, no consensus among the denominations concerning either the nature or the purpose of each order, or even how 'open' they are to all members of the *laos*. The impact of this diversity on ministerial formation is outlined in the next two sections on the diaconate and the presbyterate.

The diaconate

Deacons are ordained to the ministry of Jesus Christ. They are not ordained to a different ministry but to a different expression of the one ministry in which all Christians share. There is significant consensus in the Churches concerning the nature of the diaconate, as may be seen from the following stated vision of diaconal ministry approved by the UK Ecumenical Diaconal Consultation of 1997:

> Christ-focused, people-centred and lived out in a lifestyle both active and contemplative . . . We increasingly perceive our role to be pioneering and prophetic, responding to needs, proactive in opportunity through commitment to mission and pastoral care within and beyond the Church. Opening doors of opportunity, encouraging others to take risks, the contemporary diaconate acting in its capacity as 'agent of change', engages imaginatively and collaboratively with issues of justice, poverty, social and environmental concerns. We often find ourselves spanning boundaries, especially official ones of Church and society.[15]

Such a vision can be taken as a broad endorsement of the earlier World Council of Churches' definition of diaconal ministry:

Deacons represent to the Church its calling as servant in the world. By struggling in Christ's name with the myriad needs of societies and persons, deacons exemplify the interdependence of worship and service in Church life. They exercise responsibility in the worship of congregations: for example, by reading the scriptures, preaching and leading the people in prayer. They help in the teaching of the congregation. They exercise a ministry of love within the community. They fulfil certain administrative tasks and may be elected to responsibilities for governance.[16]

In spite of such general agreement, there remains considerable difference between denominations as to how diaconal ministry should be exercised as an ordained ministry in service to the royal priesthood, and this necessarily impacts on the training of the ordinand.

In the British Methodist Church, the diaconate is one of two parallel, complementary but distinctive orders of ministry. Deacons are called in God's name to:

- assist God's people in worship and prayer;
- hold before them the needs and concerns of the world;
- minister Christ's love and compassion;
- visit and support the sick and the suffering;
- seek out the lost and the lonely;
- help those they serve to offer their lives to God.

This description taken from the Methodist Diaconal Ordination Service has been summarized as a calling 'to exercise a ministry of witness through service in and on behalf of the Church catholic'.[17]

The Methodist Church expects a candidate for the diaconate to be called specifically to diaconal rather than presbyteral or lay ministry. It is recognized as a calling to an ordained ministry set within a religious order that has its own Rule of Life. For this reason, the training of deacons should be different from that of presbyters. It is not enough for a diaconal ordinand to know how, and on what basis, they are called to exercise their ministry as described in the ordinal; the diaconal ordinand also needs to know how and on what basis they 'belong' to a religious order and how to live according to an agreed communal Rule of Life. The distinctive form of diaconal ministry requires a correspondingly distinctive training if its particular charisms are not to be lost to the Church.

The importance of differentiating between diaconal and presbyteral pre-ordination training is less pronounced in both the Anglican and

Catholic Churches where ordination is normally sequential and cumulative. Diaconal ministry effectively serves as a form of pre-presbyteral ordination training. According to this understanding of ordained ministry, the three *munera* of teaching, governing and sanctifying, or preaching, pastoral care and sacraments, are laid upon each order, but in different degrees. The deacon has an assisting, not a presiding ministry with regard to the sacraments. According to Paul Avis:

> Deacons are sent with authority to assist the Bishop and presbyters in the ministry of word and sacrament, delivered with pastoral compassion to all who need to hear the good news and to be made whole. In relation to both clergy and people they embody and model the gospel commission that gives the Church its raison d'être.[18]

In spite of the common ground, there have always been clear distinctions between the orders which it is expected that deacons will know and honour on pain of discipline. Thus the ruling of the Council of Nicea:

> Deacons must abide within their own bounds. They shall not administer the Eucharist to Presbyters, nor touch it before Presbyters do, nor sit among the Presbyters. For all this is contrary to the canons and decent order.[19]

Sequential orders have the distinct advantage of ensuring that ordination to the presbyterate or episcopate builds on the foundation established by diaconal ordination. Paul Avis defends the tradition of sequential ordination on the basis that the earlier interpretation of the term *diakonia* as 'humble service' has now been robustly challenged on the grounds that the key texts can be read in a very different way, leading to a summary of the diaconate as a ministry which is no more general than any other ministry is, whether lay or ordained. On the contrary, it is a distinctive ministry which he claims can be elucidated by means of the traditional way of expressing the ministry of Christ, namely as 'prophet, priest and king'. If this is true then so also is his claim: 'The diaconate stands for the commissioned, mandated character of the whole Church as "sign, instrument and foretaste" of the Kingdom of God.'[20] Understood in this way, the diaconate operates as a sign to both the Church and the world which emphasizes the go-between or bridging role that all denominations concur is a part of the diaconate calling. Avis maintains that diaconal ministry is representative of the apostolic character of the whole people of God. It is, he suggests, 'a flagship ministry with significance for all Christians'.[21]

Intentionally or not, such language has the disadvantage of creating the perception that there is a hierarchy of ministry in the body of Christ which is contrary to Scripture. According to Jesus, the last shall be first, but in the sequential understanding of ordination the servant role can easily be perceived as being somehow less than the priestly role. This perception is exacerbated by the fact that during the protracted debate over women's ordination there was a time when women could be ordained to the diaconate but not to the presbyterate. The same problem persists at a different level in the Church of England today: women can now be ordained to the presbyterate but not to the episcopate.

The presbyterate

As with the diaconate, there is significant consensus concerning the presbyterate, as indicated by the following statement from the World Council of Churches:

> *Presbyters* serve as pastoral ministers of Word and sacraments in a local eucharistic community. They are preachers and teachers of the faith, exercise pastoral care, and bear responsibility for the discipline of the congregation to the end that the world may believe and that the entire membership of the Church may he renewed, strengthened and equipped in ministry. Presbyters have particular responsibility for the preparation of members for Christian life and ministry.[22]

The differences that exist between the denominations concerning presbyteral ministry are less immediately obvious than those concerning the diaconate but they are far more divisive. This is because they are less directly concerned with the 'functionality' of the ministry, the 'work' that a minister does in the Church, than with the power and authority to do the work and how that is bestowed. It is here, therefore, that the greatest distinction is to be found concerning the making or ordaining of ministers.

Gordon Kuhrt identifies two basic approaches to presbyteral ministry – the catholic and the reformed.[23] From the more catholic perspective, he states, the ordained presbyter speaks 'not only in the name of the Christian community but in the name of Christ himself in relation to the community'.[24] On this understanding, the ministry of the ordained presbyter is not derived from the community, neither is it delegated to them by the community. Quoting from the report 'Priesthood of the Ordained

Ministry', Kuhrt implies that presybyteral ministry is an appointed means whereby Christ makes his priestly sacrificial ministry present and effective to the people of God through the Word and Sacrament.[25] This understanding of priesthood is indebted to Judaism and to the Old Testament and the early Church Ecumenical Councils.

The reformed perspective would argue that the concept of a 'ministerial sacrificing priesthood' is not scriptural. The priesthood is found in the Old Testament, but not in the New. Christ's sacrifice can neither be repeated nor added to, so the sacrificial ministry is no longer necessary. At the death of Christ, the curtain of the temple was torn in two as there was no further need for a reserved holy place or a mediator between God and humanity. Christ was, and is, our great high priest who intercedes for us. The whole community of the Church rather than a particular priestly caste is called upon to minister to the world. The existence of the royal priesthood renders all individual priestly distinctions null and void. The New Testament therefore talks of presbyters rather than priests, with a special calling to proclaim the good news and heal the sick. The presbyter is a representative, not of Christ, but of the Church, the royal priesthood. Accordingly, a presbyter is 'made' by the Church through the acts of selection and training which are themselves signs of the Church's affirmation of the ordinand's calling by God to this role, all of which is celebrated and offered to God in the service of ordination. From this perspective, ordination is best described as *confirming* rather than *making* ministry.

Made by order?

Resisting the description of ordination as no more than a confirming act of the Church necessitates wrestling in the first instance with the linguistic and historical difficulties which make the development of ordination difficult to trace. The words *ordo*, *ordination* and *ordinare* do not mean the same today as they once did. *Ordo* simply meant one's state of life and *ordinare* described the process of bringing order to that state and could be used either metaphorically or politically. Even when used religiously, *ordinare* did not necessarily refer to a clerical state. Marriage and extreme unction, for example, were referred to as *ordos* until the fourteenth century.[26]

Gary Macy points out: 'the words ordination and ordinare were used to describe not only the ceremony and/or installation of bishops, priests, deacons and subdeacons but also of porters, lectors, exorcists, acolytes, canons, abbots, abbesses, kings, queens and empresses'.[27] Was it expected that these people would thereby be equipped and enabled to fulfil those callings? This is not as unlikely as might first appear when considered in the light of the importance given to the ordination of royalty by both Church and society. In the Middle Ages, those who ruled were convinced that they had been 'ordained to rule' and there is clear evidence to suggest that the populace believed in the necessity of royal ordinations. Was this out of superstitious fear, or does it testify to a real belief in the ability of the rite of ordination to do more than publicly confirm the succession?

Regardless of the historical vagaries surrounding the various practices of ordination during the Middle Ages, many in the Church remain convinced that there is an efficacy in ordination, testified to by experience and supported by a profound Trinitarian theology of being and belonging, which flows like a scarlet thread from the cross to the present day. Each ordination is a divine act of the Triune God. It is a sacrament in that it constitutes an outward and visible sign of the inward, invisible grace of God bestowed on the whole Church through the creation of a minister of the gospel and apostle of Christ. God the Father 'pre-ordains' someone to a particular form of ministry, God the Son incarnates, authorizes and exemplifies that ministry, and God the Holy Spirit equips and enables the ministry to fulfil its divine purpose. As with all acts of the Trinity, it is unhelpful to think of it in either purely functional or sequential terms. The call of God does not end with ordination, any more than the example that Christ set can be said to have ended with his death on the cross or the work of the Holy Spirit to have only begun after Christ's resurrection.

Ordination considered as a divine act poses at least three different types of theological questions. First, there are the ontological issues. What does it mean that someone is elected or pre-ordained by God to be an ordained minister? How does ordination change a person's character or identity – and for how long? Second, there are the incarnational, functional and practical issues. What does ordination require of the *laos* and of the ordained person? What is it that can only be done by an ordained person, and why? What authority does ordination have, and how is it used? Third, there are the spiritual or sacramental issues. What is the inward grace signified by ordination? What is uniquely given by God in ordination? How does ordination affect the individual abilities and charisms of the minister?

The ordinal of each tradition carries the particular denominational answers to most, if not all, of the above questions in liturgical form, as the purpose of such liturgy is to rehearse the Trinitarian act that it commemorates and celebrates. It would be inappropriate to attempt to explicate and then compare the implicit and explicit theologies carried by these services for each of the main denominations, as this presumes that ordination can be separated out of the understanding of Christian discipleship – something that would be vehemently denied by all concerned. Every ordination begins with the call of God to the whole people of God, both lay and those already ordained, to witness and participate in the celebration and affirmation of what God is doing in creation.

In what follows, therefore, I propose to examine each of the three different sorts of questions paying particular attention to new and/or emergent ministries and seriously to consider what it means in such instances to say that a minister is ordained rather than made.

Ontological questions

Many ministers are convinced that the whole purpose of their life is to serve Christ as a minister of the gospel. They would have no difficulty in accepting the idea that they had been pre-ordained to ministry before they had even been born. Paul, however, is quite clear in his letters of the equality of the elect who are predestined. For all whom Christ has called, he has also pre-ordained. Nonetheless, Paul's own story of ministerial development provides an excellent illustration of the value of transferable skills to ordained ministry. Paul's life prior to his encounter with Christ on the road to Damascus was already given in service to the God of Israel. The evidence suggests that he persecuted the embryonic Church out of zeal for Judaism and for the one true God. His commitment to Christ once the truth had been revealed to him was a continuation of his original calling. Ministerial training can often be so disruptive of life for the ordinand that the continuity of their calling is difficult to recognize. The Church has so far had a somewhat limited view of transferable skills and has, on the whole, lacked the imagination to develop training for ordination based on an additive rather than subtractive model. Pre-ordination training is deemed necessary to correct a lack in the ordinand's knowledge rather than in order to build on what God has already done. The move towards part-time training has made a significant contribution in helping the Church to recognize that pre-ordination means that God has already been active in the life of the minister in ways that should not be either dismissed or devalued.

Continuity of calling does not preclude the possibility of ordination effecting an ontological change; it does, however, imply that ordination is best understood as meaning the ongoing act of being and becoming a minister of God's grace by God's grace, rather than the service at which a person is publicly set aside to hold a particular office in the Church. In the same way that baptism remains effective throughout the lifetime of the Christian, so too the service of ordination is a sign of God's continuing grace. It rehearses God's lasting covenant with the Church as the gathered people of God, as well as God's promise for the future of all creation. In the service, the Church celebrates the faithfulness of God in raising up ministers. In affirming the worth of those to be ordained, the Church declares its trust in the promise that God will, if asked, provide sufficient grace to enable the minister to bear the awesome responsibility of administering the means of grace to others. Luther's and Calvin's insistence that the ordained minister does not undergo an ontological change but remains a member of the *laos* needs to be set alongside the fact that *every* relationship is transformative. When a woman and a man get married, for example, they undergo a profound ontological change that is not occasioned by the vows or the service, but by the change in relationship which the service signifies. It is not only their identity that changes, but who they are, before God and in the eyes of the world. In the course of the marriage, the two will become one; this is a change of essence, not just of character or name.

The same is true of ordination. The ordained person and the Church are both changed by the grace that flows from God as a consequence of the new relationship that they entered into through ordination. The identity of the minister is changed in a way which is not revoked, even when the person changes the context of, or ceases to practise the 'functions' of, ordained ministry.[28] Even in those Protestant traditions which deny the ontological efficacy of ordination, it is still largely believed that ordination is permanent and cannot be undone. The nature of the relationship of the minister with the ordaining Church may change, but not the fact of their ordination because ordination is first and foremost an affirmation of what God has done, not what the Church has achieved.

Incarnational questions

The incarnation was not accidental; it occurred at a specific time, at a specific place in order that God's plan could be fulfilled. John's Gospel describes it in terms of Christ coming 'to his own' and of his being sent 'in the fullness of time'. Much that has been said about fresh expressions and emerging church ministry is similarly incarnational. It is a ministry to a particular people at a particular time with the same divine purpose of reconciliation. It is therefore first and foremost a highly specific ministry, not only in terms of its practice but in terms of its location and timing.

The question of whether pioneer ministers are made by the Church to meet an identified need regarding mission, or pre-ordained by God to serve a particular divine purpose, is shown as a false dichotomy when the ministry is set in its appropriate incarnational context. Christ did not come from outside of Judaism, but was born as a son of David. Neither did he ignore or neglect the synagogue. He was initiated into Judaism through his circumcision, learned the Torah and read it before the gathered people. He was a regular worshipper at both synagogue and temple, and clearly kept the feasts of the Jewish Calendar. His criticism of the religious leaders of the day was neither universal nor as dismissive as selective supersessionist readings have led many to believe. It should not surprise us therefore when pioneer ministers are similarly raised up out of the people of God. They are members of the Church, initiated into it by their baptism, well versed in the Scriptures; preachers and teachers who have learned to share in the prayer and worship of the Church. They are familiar with the Christian Calendar, and in addition to their own private devotions celebrate the main festivals with other Christians in churches and cathedrals. Their vocal criticism of the Church of today is not universal, neither is it intended to destroy the Church – but rather to renew the body of Christ.

Set in this context, it is easier to recognize that the changes to training patterns and selection criteria for ordained pioneer ministers are not an attempt to create a ministry to serve the present age; rather, they form part of the Church's response, drawing on centuries of revealed wisdom, to strengthen and support the work that God has already begun. Without exception, every generation since the time of Christ has experienced its own 'fresh expression' of Church, yet the demands of ministry have remained the same. All ministers are ordained to an incarnational ministry, to proclaim the gospel so that it can be heard and responded to, to teach the doctrines of the Church so that the truth can be known, to administer the sacraments and to watch over one another in love; but above all, to participate in the reconciling, healing love of God.

An incarnational ministry requires the laity to be willing to follow the often rather unorthodox leadership of the one ordained. A high degree of trust is entailed, but it is trust that should be earned rather than solely given in faith. Although Jesus did not perform signs for signs' sake, he did provide evidence of the authenticity of his ministry, not least through his knowledge of the Scriptures and his devotional life. Ordination thus requires that ordinands be willing to make their calling evident by the way in which they live their life, their knowledge of and commitment to the

Gospel and their obedience to God. Signs and wonders may accompany their ministry, but these should always point to the work of Christ. Their ministry will be conducted among the particular people that they have been called to serve, but as a result of God's grace, pioneer ministers may develop a 'following', drawing crowds with their preaching and their outreach. A characteristic of ordained ministry, however, is that, like Christ, ministers will direct 'their' following to the kingdom, refusing to take the glory for themselves.

Through the parable of the vineyard (Luke 20.9–19) and other teachings, Jesus stressed that he was not the first to call people to God. Though unique, he nonetheless chose to associate himself with the long line of prophets. In the same way, every ordained minister belongs to a succession of ministers who have proclaimed the same message of repentance, reconciliation and obedience to God. The 'apostolic succession' is not merely a succession of church officers stretching back to the time of Peter; it is a succession of all those whom God has ordained to participate in the ministry of reconciliation. The symbolic act of the laying on of hands in ordination is just one of the signs of this continuity. It is reminiscent of the blessing and endowment that a father traditionally gave to his heir. While the sign is not essential (there is no indication, for example, that Jesus received such a sign), what it signifies is essential. The continuity of proclamation through time is an important witness to the constancy of God's love and action in the world.

Christ's ministry is set in the context of the salvation of all God's people. By his life, death, resurrection and ascension he introduced a permanent change in the way in which the good news of God's love and grace to the world is re-presented. The one who proclaimed the good news, became the good news. Incarnational ministry demands the same of every ordained person. They are not only to represent the good news of God's unfailing love and mercy, they are to be good news to the world. This is the heart of the incarnational representational nature of the one ordained.

Ordained ministers re-present Christ to the world, not *as* Christ, but by being as conformed to the image of Christ as is humanly and divinely possible by the grace of God. They also re-present the Church to the world as the foretaste of the kingdom. In both these tasks, those who are ordained share in the ministry of the whole people of God. Incarnational ministry demands one further form of representation from those who are ordained, namely that as Christ represented humanity through his kenotic obedience to the will of the Father, 'even unto death', so they also should seek to represent the Church and the world to God. They are called to empty themselves of personal ambition, and instead to offer up the 'collect' of all God's people, to intercede for them, as one who loves them and who is prepared to give up everything for them, 'that they might have life in all its fullness'. This threefold representational ministry finds its fullest expression in the sacraments of baptism and the Eucharist.

The representational nature of ministry makes the question of authority very important. By what authority does the ordained minister presume to represent the Church and the world to God, or God to the Church and the world? Christ's authority was given to him by God. He then gave the disciples authority to heal the sick, cast out demons and proclaim the good news. Later on, Paul records how the authority for his ministry was given to him by Christ. A naïve interpretation of Scripture would thus seem to imply that those who are ordained receive their authority from God and not the Church. But Christ also taught respect for the authority of the law and for the gathered community. Scripture also records how, following the ascension, the disciples apparently shared responsibility for ministry, seeking the mind of Christ in the consensus of the community.

The early Church's wrestling with the question of personal over communal authority is writ large in the Acts of the Apostles and in the epistles. Personal revelations were brought before the community, especially if they implied a change in the shared understanding of what to teach or do. Thus Peter, for example, explained to the other disciples not only that it was permissible to eat what had previously been declared 'unclean', but why. Similarly, it is precisely because Paul's ministry was from Christ that Paul accepted the authority of the Council at Jerusalem concerning where and to whom he could mission, and what he should teach. Now, as then, authority to minister is given by Christ, through the Church.

Spiritual questions

The Moravian Faith and Order summary of the reformed perspective on ordination as the authority to perform certain ministerial functions on behalf of the Church is an oversimplification. The idea that God will provide a minister with every gift and charism that the Church has historically deemed necessary for ordained ministry is neither scripturally nor experientially sound. Ordination training can assist in providing some of the basic skills for preaching, pastoral care and presidency at the sacraments, but ministry cannot be reduced to a set of core skills. Most ordinands are familiar with the experience of having worked hard to prepare what they believe will be an inspiring act of worship, only to have it all fall flat. Without the activity of grace, a sermon, no matter how well written or delivered, is just a monologue – sometimes interesting, sometimes entertaining, often boring, but never inspiring. Ordination is the offer of God's grace. It is an invitation to ordinands to work with God, to allow God to supply whatever is lacking, not to make them a better preacher or pastoral visitor, but to make the ministry that they offer effective. In order to respond to that offer of grace, ordained ministers need to cultivate the spiritual gifts that enable them to discern the will of God for the people of God.

The spiritual gifts needed are basically the same as those that are needed by all Christians to fulfil their calling to grow in grace and holiness. All forms of ordination training therefore need to nurture the spiritual growth of the ordinand. The tendency to see training only in terms of learning outcomes and practical competencies is dangerous in that it appears to reduce ministry to its function and ignore the importance of its character. The ordinands' relationship with God is crucial to their ministry, yet this is hard to evaluate in terms of competencies and outcomes. Similarly, the devotional life of ordinands, their commitment to prayer, worship and the study of the Scriptures, is essential; yet as these are generally conducted in private, they are similarly almost impossible to assess. One of the few remaining advantages of residential seminaries over part-time courses for ministerial training is the opportunity that they provide for detailed observation of the ordinands' spiritual life. The disadvantage is that the observations are unlikely to be an accurate record of the real spiritual life of most of the ordinands. The seminary is too artificial an environment for the vast majority of today's ordinands. It was designed with single young men in mind, not married middle-aged men and women. The unnatural return to 'student' life with its attendant financial difficulties, coupled with the awareness of being 'observed' and 'assessed', places a real stress on spiritual growth and formation. Training on courses may not provide the same opportunities for direct observation by the course staff, but it has the distinct advantage of locating the spiritual growth of the ordinand in the heart of the sponsoring community. It encourages the ordinand to make the connection between everyday life and spiritual life and to seek to develop those gifts which will enable them to actively transform the secular into the sacred.

The particular gift of grace that is reserved for the ordained minister is the gift of sacramental character. The role that the ordained minister has in the celebration of the Eucharist is a means of grace to both the minister and the communicant. For the minister, the grace that is bestowed is the freedom to participate in the moment when sign and divine reality interact and heaven and earth are united. It is a grace of immense power and transformative potential. It is also a relational grace defining the minister by virtue of their standing in heaven and on earth, before God and with the people of God. Sacramental character is the unique gift of grace given through ordination. It is not the power to preside, nor even the authority to preside, but the wherewithal to join with God in making a moment, and thereby a people, holy.

Ordination training can only partially prepare the ordinand to preside at the Eucharist. The study of liturgy and worship, of the meaning of sacraments and the gifts of grace, all help the ordinand to know how to break the bread and lift the cup when the moment comes, but an ordinand cannot be trained in how to 'be' holy, only in how to practise holiness. It is possible for an ordinand to learn how to mimic the sacred character, but true holiness and the wherewithal to join with God in making a moment and a people holy is a gift of grace, for all that it is a highly desirable learning outcome of every ordination course.

Made in order that . . .

> When I am frightened by what I am to you, then I am consoled by what I am with you. To you I am the bishop, with you I am a Christian. The first is an office, the second a grace; the first a danger, the second salvation.[29]

This chapter has explored the extent to which ministers are made by the Church for circuit and parish ministry through the processes of selection and training and ordained by God to the work of the kingdom. It has shown that mission and ecclesial context and expectations inevitably do shape ministers for particular orders. Viewed negatively, the processes by which ministers are selected and trained for ordination can be interpreted as manipulative and controlling, with ministerial training collaborating by churning out regularized diaconal or presbyteral ministers to order, according to some set menu for the day. Viewed positively, those same processes can be recognized as the Church working synergistically with God in moulding those whom God has called in order that they are better able to serve the needs of the age.

The making and the ordaining of ministers is, at best, an integrated process which enables those who are called to ordained ministry to grow beyond the expectations of either themselves or others. In spite of the difficulties of every age, it is evident that God's grace does not work simply to address or counter the effects of the Church. God works in and through the Church, providing the strength, ability, charity and humility for ministers to become more Christlike. The seal of Christ's approval granted at ordination liberates ministers to be fully who they are before God and with the people of God through the means of grace administered by the Church. It is the time when the minister hears and understands the prophetic words, 'I have called you by name, you are mine' (Isaiah 43.1).

Notes

1 Stewart Mills, 'Clergymen, Gentlemen and Men: World War I and the Requirements, Recruitment and Training of the Anglican Ministry', *Dutch Review of Church History*, 83:1, 2003, pp. 435–47.

2 As recounted in Mills, 'Clergymen, Gentlemen and Men'.

3 Mills, 'Clergymen, Gentlemen and Men'.

4 Mills, 'Clergymen, Gentlemen and Men', p. 447.

5 http://www.acpi.org.uk/downloads/Ordained_Pioneer_Ministers_ Guidelines.pdf, December 2007.

6 http://www.acpi.org.uk/downloads/Ordained_Pioneer_Ministers_ Guidelines.pdf, December 2007.

7 John Macquarrie, *Principles of Christian Theology*, London: SCM Press, 1966, p. 380.

8 Macquarrie, *Principles of Christian Theology*, p. 381.

9 Jan Kerkhofs, 'From Frustration to Liberation: A Factual Approach to Ministries in the Church', in Lucas Grollenberg et al. (eds), *Minister, Pastor, Prophet: Grass Roots Leadership in the Church*, London: SCM Press, 1980, p. 20.

10 The *Codex Iuris Canonici*, canon 1024, with regard to ordination read: 'only a baptised male receives ordination validly'. As quoted in Michael Slusser, 'The Ordination of Male Infants', *Theological Studies*, 57:2, 1996, pp. 313–17.

11 H. Noldin, *Summa Theologiae Moralis iuxta Codieem Iuris Canonici*, 30th edn. A. Schmitt and Godefridus Heinzel (eds), Innsbruck: Feliciani Rauch, 1954, 3.399–400, quoted in Slusser, 'The Ordination of Male Infants'.

12 *Codicis Iuris Canonicai Fontes*, ed. Peter Gasparri, Rome: Typis Polygottis Vaticanis, 1937, pp. 894–903, quoted in Slusser, 'The Ordination of Male Infants'.

13 First Council of Nicea, AD 325, canons 15 and 16.

14 The United Methodist Church consecrates bishops, but not to a separate order. Bishops of the United Methodist Church remain a part of the order of elders, i.e. presbyters.

15 *The Windsor Statement on the Diaconate*, 1997, produced at MDO Centre, 26 St James Road, Edgbaston, Birmingham. The Church of Scotland, the Episcopal Church in Scotland, the British Methodist Church, the Roman Catholic Church and the Church of England were represented at the meeting. Conversations also included church-related community workers from the United Reformed Church and an Orthodox deacon in training.

16 *Baptism, Eucharist and Ministry*, Geneva: World Council of Churches, 1982, M31, p. 27.

17 Methodist Church, 'What is a Deacon?', 2004, http://www.methodist.org. uk/index.cfm/fuseaction=information.content&cmid=883, 2008.

18 Paul Avis, 'The Revision of the Ordinal in the Church of England 1550–2005', *Ecclesiology*, 1:2, 2005, pp. 95–110.

19 First Council of Nicea, AD 325, canon 18.

20 Avis, 'The Revision of the Ordinal'.

21 Avis, 'The Revision of the Ordinal'.

22 *Baptism, Eucharist and Ministry*, M30, p. 27.

23 Gordon Wilfred Kuhrt, *An Introduction to Christian Ministry: Following Your Vocation in the Church of England*, London: Church House Publishing, 2000.

24 Kuhrt, *An Introduction to Christian Ministry*, p. 55.

25 Kuhrt, *An Introduction to Christian Ministry*, p. 55.

26 See Gary Macy, 'The Ordination of Women in the Early Middle Ages', *Theological Studies*, 61:3, 2000, pp. 481–503.

27 Macy, 'The Ordination of Women'.

28 Historically, ordination was not thought to be irreversible until the thirteenth century. Before this time, if a deacon or a priest fell from grace in some way he could be deposed and later reordained if he recanted his heresy. The concept of ordination as a permanent, indelible sign of God's grace was not directly affirmed by either the Church's teaching or practice until the fifteenth and sixteenth centuries.

29 Augustine, Sermons 349 I PL 38, 1483.

Part 2

Formed in Ministry

5

Professional, Purposeful, Ecclesial and Liturgical:
The Link with Tradition

KENNETH WILSON

Introduction

When I went up to university in 1957, I remember how important many
undergraduates thought it was to keep their distance in order to be themselves. For example, I recall many an undergraduate who, when invited by
the college representative to join the Methodist Society, would coyly
respond, 'Well, I may; let's see how things go.' And *sotto voce* one could
almost hear the further sentence, 'In any case, my ideas are so significant
and so important to me that I'm sure they will not fit into your conversation or possibly even make sense to you.' It was as if they had original
ideas that they were sure no one would have thought of before, and therefore they needed time to think them through by themselves before taking
them into the public domain. I'm inclined to take the same view of many
of those who come up with so-called new initiatives in ministry, ministerial formation and church governance. The liquid Church, house
churches, fresh expressions, are not new. Actually there is nothing new
under the sun; all these contemporary so-called experiments have their
parallels in history, though the form and means whereby we experience
the realities that underlie the faith may well fluctuate from generation to
generation and from place to place. Wesley's open-air preaching has no
meaningful place in the contemporary Western world, but we have not yet
come up with a satisfactory alternative which could have an analogous
impact as a means whereby to woo the world into conversation.

Information technology is changing our means of communication with
unprecedented speed, but it has not yet matured sufficiently to provide a
meaningful substitute for the real presence implicit in personal conversation. Certainly there seems little sense in a *virtual* Church, any more
than there is in a *virtual* conversation, and perhaps for the same reason.
For one thing, it suggests that it can exist in the ether freestanding and

unconnected, with no awareness of any historical tradition. Ignorance of the personal human past in which to place the images presented and in terms of which to make sense of them renders them meaningless. This can only be countered by personal interaction and the face-to-face conversation that goes with it. I do not question that basic information can be efficiently stored and transferred by means of information technology. However, there is no substitute for the open, intriguing and demanding presence of a person to bring about the necessary relationship if genuine learning is to take place. Every teacher and parent is well aware of this, though the cultural assumptions implicit in our current socio-economic and political structures make it difficult to achieve this, notwithstanding the growing evidence to support it. Without awareness of the traditions in which we stand as human beings, we are lost. But what do we mean by tradition?

Tradition

I am loath to talk of *the* tradition, though in principle I should like to. On the one hand I realize that for many, tradition smacks of being old-fashioned and out of date, but such a judgement completely misses the point. As a matter of fact, tradition is the *living* account we give of where we have come from which helps us to recognize where we stand, on the basis of which we shall determine which of the many possible futures opened up we elect for. Then, again for many, to talk of *the* tradition is to limit our freedom. Surely there are many traditions? Indeed there are, but for the Christian believer, all of them concern one single tradition of reflection and enquiry that is focused on God – Father, Son and Holy Spirit. The Church, the community of faith, is where the presence of the risen Christ is celebrated, the *ur*-tradition is remembered, and conversation with the real presence of our Lord realized. This conversation is not a simple matter: it is a rich experience stimulated by the Holy Spirit involving all that we know, all that we are, all that we can be and all the insight we can muster. It is a lifetime experience of change, for we are not only to become members of the tradition, but part of it and capable of developing it for ourselves. Nothing passive, old-fashioned, out of date or irrelevant about that!

One might put it like this. Human society from its very beginning, say 150,000 years ago, has struggled to make sense of the world, to discover the place of human being in the nature of things, and to become aware of the fundamental assumptions that lie behind any and every explanation that is proposed. And, of course, there is then the fundamental business of investigating the trustworthiness, even the truth – if we are bold enough to use the term – of those assumptions. As Aristotle said, we are the *curious* people – we want to know. In our minds there has always been associated with a natural fear of the unknown an equally natural absolute delight and thrill in the chase of enquiring: the tentative confidence that leads us to appreciate with boldness the beauty, order and seemingly essential predictability of the processes with which we are involved. For the Christian, this amounts to nothing less than *love* of the world.

It is a fact that we can only learn if we cultivate the art of enquiry with the necessary detachment and honesty; for this to develop it is essential that we love the object of our enquiry. To despise a race, a nation, a culture, is to imply that it is not worth attention and therefore to exclude it from our love. Sadly, in human history this has too often been the case; when that happens it is not so much the race or the gender that is diminished, but the persons who have rationed their capacity to love. Indeed, to love is precisely to want the well-being of the object of one's love, to pay attention to and serve its best interests, whether that be the rainforest, a favourite hammer, a nation, a friend, a culture, a spouse, or the world, or whatever. Or, of course, God!

This realization underlines all the more coherently the importance of curiosity as an expression of our human nature. For it is only by studying, paying attention to what one loves, that one will learn what is involved in trying to secure the well-being of our friend. To the extent that we are focused on ourselves, we shall fail to live up to the stated ambition to love 'the other'.

The naturalness of the desire that we find in ourselves to want to love, that is to 'give ourselves to the attempt to secure the well-being of the other', has led Christians to become aware of God, the Creative Redeemer of all that is, was and is to be. We sense with moral certainty that the love we have for 'the other' is not self-generated, but dependent upon the generous self-giving of the other – not the world itself, but God who is the origin and end of all that is. We love because God first loved us. God is not 'behind' the world as if God was no more than an explanation of how the world came into existence; God is that personal presence, awareness of whom in Christ establishes the ground of the love that we find in ourselves for the world and for one another.

Of course, it does not always seem like that: there are serious issues to take into account. We call them problems, but in fact they are stimuli to further thought, and to the deepening of our ability and willingness to love. There are the many problems of evil that range from natural disasters to the consequences of the moral turpitude of human beings, including us. Some of these are due to our ignorance, others to sheer stupidity. Even earthquakes may one day be predictable, and in any case we could choose to build in places where earthquakes are less likely, and use materials that are more resistant to shock. We have to struggle against laziness, ignorance and complacency. Perhaps ignorance is the greatest of the problems that we face, especially the profound ignorance that lies behind overconfidence and an unwillingness to think that we have anything more to learn.

Utopias are grounded in such ignorance. People who *know* what is going on will be determined (of course for the ultimate good of all!) to force others to follow them if persuasion is ineffective, and, as they see it, the truth is ignored. Such people are a menace. If they believe that they have the authority of God for what they are doing because of some position that they hold, or some personal word vouchsafed to them alone by God, they are not only wrong but live in denial of their human nature. Dubiety is the stimulus to further knowledge, to deeper self-awareness, and a necessary condition if we are to recognize what it is to love the other and secure its long-term interests. Ultimately our focus must therefore be on God, whose nature is love. This is not instead of focusing on the world, but in order the better to have the courage to open ourselves in love of the world and thus to share in God's eternal redemptive creation of the world.

The ultimate evil, it seems, is death, in comparison with which all other evils are as nothing. However, it all depends on the world that we are making whether the recent prediction that 50 per cent of those who are 30 years of age at the moment could well live to the age of 100 is a welcome or daunting thought. There is for the Christian – and indeed for people of faith who are part of the other major religions of the world – a fate worse than death. Christians call it *hell*, which we may for the sake of argument describe as a condition of absolute irredeemable loneliness and separation. For the Christian, therefore, a life of 100 years may be welcome, but it is not the be-all and end-all, because to know and love God is to realize that since God is love, one's present and therefore one's future are in God's hands. It is Jesus whom we call the Christ, the Son of God, whose incarnation, teaching, sacrificial death, resurrection and ascension illuminate both the nature of God and the nature of humankind. God – Father, Son and Holy Spirit – is committed to our well-being. What that means for us and for the world takes a lifetime to explore.

I referred above to the one tradition in which we stand: this is it. But our tradition is remarkable, despite all evidence to the contrary, for its openness and affective interest. This is because it grows out of and is not apart from the natural human search for meaning which itself owes its origin to God, the Holy Spirit. Therefore the Christian tradition can afford to be curious about and alive to the whole world of God's creation, the history of human culture and enquiry. Indeed, our tradition's strength is drawn from the fact that it is so: its history is not one of inviolable purity, but of growth and development through a complex creative interaction with all human enquiry. It is no accident that we want to know about the natural world of which we are an aspect, to understand it and apply what we learn by means of technological innovation. Insofar as we use our knowledge wisely, and keep the consequences under review, we are sharing in God's redemptive creativity. The same may be said for all other specialist disciplines in the arts and sciences, both physical and social.

Above all, therefore, far from being fearful about other religious traditions of enquiry as they appear, for example, in Hinduism, Buddhism, Judaism and Islam, we want to pay attention to them, and, because of the nature of our faith, we can afford to do so. As Jacques Dupuis SJ has argued, and more recently Fr Peter Phan has suggested, they would not exist in God's world were it not the case that they have something to teach us.

In our complex, overcrowded world, where the basic resources of energy, clean air, water and land are in short supply, the foundational religious beliefs of humankind have a crucial role to play in our future human flourishing. There is no future for the human race if religious traditions hold themselves apart from one another and engage in a power struggle for domination, as if it was conceivable that somehow one of them would triumph by destroying the others. Truth and wisdom are not the products of the exercise of power but of authority, and that can only be achieved through understanding and sensitive respect for the truth, wherever it is to be found. Surely we have got beyond the stage of believing that the purpose of the Church and of Christian faith is to convert the world if that means making everyone a believing Christian?

The Christian understanding of conversion is much less confined and restrictive; a world converted will be a world where all people, as it were, face the same direction and in so doing work together for the long-term well-being of the whole of creation and the human race in particular. This will not be the achievement of one religion or one philosophy; Christians are not going to do this on their own. In the light of growing human response-ability our task is to contribute with others to an emerging situation where human society becomes more responsible for God's creation, for the world's sake and in full knowledge of the reality of God's presence with God's people. And by 'God's people', Christians do mean *all* people. Of all the major religions, this is a responsibility that the Christian tradition can undertake without fear, because it is an essential feature of our faith that God is redemptively creative. By which we mean that God first committed God's self to the whole of God's creation to inspire it and renew it, not exclusively to the Church. The Church exists for the sake of the world, not the world for the sake of the Church.

Ecclesia

The Church is the community of faith, called into being by Christ: he is the head of the Church and presides over all its affairs. The work of the Church is to give attention to God on behalf of the whole creation and all humankind. It celebrates in worship God's presence in Christ, and with the assistance of the Holy Spirit seeks to establish what this means for our public understanding of the world, our relationship with it, and its significance for our own lives. The quest is never ending, infinitely intriguing, always puzzling, but ultimately satisfying. Its success depends upon our willingness to assist one another in drawing on all the available disciplines of human enquiry. The result is an enhanced capacity to make judgements about the best ways for us to act, both as communities and as persons in community. How we go about the business of making judgements is crucial to the likelihood of their success. But since no enquiry comes to an end, all judgements are provisional and subject to adaptation or rejection in the light of experience.

The Christian is well aware that 'here there is no continuing city', both in the sense of the temporary nature of this world of space and time, and more particularly of the provisionality of the world picture which is presented to our minds as the result of our present knowledge and experience. The Church's task is to maintain a nice balance between what we think we know and how we think we should proceed in order to learn more. This is a comment on our humanity, our human nature – not simply on progress in physics, biochemistry, history or psychology. All these enquiries as they mature raise questions for us about our humanity and our selves. As members of the Church we are part of a community that has been delivered into the freedom of Christ and encouraged to enquire with confidence. And a good thing too! A Church protective of itself and closed to new knowledge is, like a closed mind, a contradiction in terms. Openness is a defining characteristic of what it is to be a Church, as it is of what constitutes a mind. To be focused on God, which is what the Church must essentially be, implies that the Christian mind and spirit is constantly challenged to become more receptive to truth.

How does one begin to share in the life of the Christian community? In the minds of some who discuss the matter, there is a special way into the faith. For some, that would be conversion – a sudden overwhelming personal experience of the presence of the living God. For others, it would be the formal celebration of the sacrament of baptism. For yet others it is a product of casual conversation with a friend, which they might call the work of the Holy Spirit. Then again, there are those like the poet Edwin Muir. He, when working for the British Council in Prague, simply came to the realization while putting on his trousers that, unrecognized by himself, he had been a Christian all his life. Getting started on any enterprise is often a mysterious business. For myself, it seems pointless to look for '*the* way in'. The fact is that, when once we have become aware of our curiosity about the nature of things, we have begun the process. When was I not curious? I cannot remember a time, but then I take the view that my curiosity must have pre-existed my awareness of what it is to be curious.

What then needs to be added if this natural curiosity is to be brought into the Christian community's conversation with Jesus is an occasion when one realizes what is going on and wants formally and constructively to take responsibility for oneself. To remember or be reminded that we have been baptized may raise the question of what it means. To be required to read chunks of the Bible in order to make sense of Milton may introduce a person into the tradition. To be puzzled about free will when studying the sciences may stimulate wider reflection on the nature of the relationship between theological enquiry, philosophical investigation and the scientific method. To be the beneficiary of marvellous sacrificial acts of kindness may prompt the question, 'Why?'. To be taken to a Eucharist when staying with friends may touch a chord that resonates for evermore. Who knows?

What is certain is that we will need the support of a worshipping community of faith if our curiosity is to be kept alive. I realize that this is not how most members, let alone those who look into the Christian tradition from outside, seem to regard the community of faith. For them, to be a Christian is to evince ignorance, to be possessed of a closed mind and to have withdrawn from the real world out of fear. Nothing could be further from the truth. Liberty, openness and freedom of thought are the marks of true faith. Hence my assertion that we share in the life of the Church not to hide from reality but in order to ensure that our curiosity in the human condition is constantly aroused; indeed, the last thing which participation in the life of a worshipping Christian community will or should provide is security and certainty: actually there is no such condition open to us as human beings. Certainties are fatal and destructive of faith; indeed, they are to all human life. To be regularly reminded in worship of the Christian claims about God, the Holy Trinity and God's omnipotent, all-loving presence when we are only too well aware of human suffering surely keeps alive one's curiosity. We are surrounded by dis-order, dis-ease, hunger, treachery, fear, not to mention the bombastic demands of dysfunctional, ignorant seekers after personal power: they are always with us. Far from putting them aside when we enter church, we take them into the presence of God when we worship and we are forced to *think*! What does this all mean? To celebrate God's presence in the real world is to become more aware of the world as it is, *and* of the love of God for it which demanded, demands and receives God's all. And also, of course, it confirms one's determination to work with God to understand the world better so as to be able, with others, to share in God's redemptive creativity.

There is a great deal of talk at the moment of the Church's need for better governance, by which most people mean better management. This is nowhere more to the fore than in Methodism. There is certainly plenty of waste: as we are often told, if a business made as little use of its assets as the Church does, bankruptcy would stare it in the face. The answer of church authorities seems to be more centralization and the development of tiers of middle management to bridge the gap between the centre and the local church. There is no doubt that a middle tier of management will be busy, because like any bureaucracy those in post have to find work to do in order to justify their existence. However, most of the work they do is unnecessary and deskills those 'below' them who have the experience and personal authority. This tendency is all a great mistake since it confuses the Church as material substance (buildings, reporting procedures, performance indicators, compliance with government legislation, effective financial arrangements, etc., all of which have of course their importance) with the vital life of the community of faith. As we recognize from experience elsewhere, all the church structures could be enhanced with the apparent appearance of better government, without achieving the slightest impact on the real life of faith.

The community of faith is quite different. It emerges from the conversation that Christ began with his disciples; it is dependent upon the tradition for which there is also biblical witness, and builds upon its continuing lively experience. It is focused upon the Triune God, upon truth, justice, peace and mutual affection that are all impossible to manage. They have no place on a balance sheet and cannot be computed. The attempt to record real success when reporting achievements on a form enquiring about publicly accountable indicators has frustrated many a headteacher when he or she is attempting to 'make a difference' in the school. A minister may suffer the same frustration and be diminished because the designated performance indicators domesticate thought, control ideas and define the indefinable. And as we well know, a management culture leads some personalities whom we choose to assume responsibility for the life of the Church to protect themselves and secure their own interests by personal aggrandizement rather than by cultivating the exercise of a mutual authority under God in Christ. The consequence is that a false authority is assumed which it is impossible to exercise because it is not really accepted, and which is inimical to the well-being of the community of faith as well as to the personal faith of individuals. For, let us be quite clear, in the case of the Christian, faith takes priority over religion.

Is the minister a member of a profession?

Yes, but the minister is not limited to a professional role, the terms and conditions of which can be written down in a contract. To be a minister or priest is in one sense, but only in one limited sense, to be a professional. The sense in which a minister is a professional is not unimportant; indeed, if this role is performed badly it affects everything else which lies at the heart of the matter. So, despite my remarks above about managerialism in church affairs, it is essential that ministers accept their duty to be professional in the conduct of the business of the Church. It may be, indeed it should be, that there are other professional persons better qualified than a minister is, willing and able to undertake the duties and responsibilities of finance, property and employment. However, even when that is successfully achieved, it is the minister's professional job to see that it is all done well.

Over and above, and underpinning this, what lies at the heart of the minister's vocation is what he or she is, not what he or she does. The priest or minister is the person who represents our Lord as the president of the celebration of the Holy Communion, the Lord's Supper, which we increasingly refer to as the Eucharist. I put this at the centre of the minister's life because it is from the authority that flows from the presidency of the sacrament that all other responsibilities flow. It is to this representative role that ministers are ordained: it is what ordination means and what makes it so humiliating, yet enervating. The minister, as the representative of Christ, presides at the sacrament of which Christ himself is the eternal celebrant. The minister breaks the bread and pours the cup of wine. They, the body and blood of Christ, are shared with the whole congregation (which, of course, includes the minister) who themselves represent the world of creation and all people, for God in Christ is alive for the whole world, not just for Christians.

As the president of the congregation that receives Christ on behalf of the whole world, it should dawn on us that we had better do something to make a reality of it. We can't just take God's gift away and put it in the cupboard until next time, like the unadventurous recipient of the single talent. Nor can we presume upon the gift and try to take it out on the rest of the world whom we may consider less privileged or fortunate than ourselves. After all, we are now secure – so they had better pay up! The 'unjust steward' should be a lesson to us all.

So, in as gentle and persuasive a way as possible, the minister should lead the community of faith to enquire into the nature of the world and our human experience of it. Given that we celebrate the presence of God with God's people – by which Christians mean all people – and that we believe that there are sufficient talents for us all to benefit from the interest which accrues, minds to employ in unpacking the secrets of the physical world, and hearts to sympathize with those who appear to be excluded, we would do well to get on with the job. There are enough resources, enough goodwill, and sufficient concern if we direct them in the right ways. We will identify the human failure implicit in our jealousies, greed and indifference; we shall be able to point to some of the institutional structures that get in the way, and we shall begin to see where we should invest for the best returns in human welfare.

However, if we are honest, we shall be overwhelmed by the task. It is more than I can do by myself; it is more than my congregation can achieve; it is beyond all Christians even if we were united (some hope!). There are no simple or single solutions. Indeed, any progress will be likely to produce side-effects. Thus, let's get rid of child poverty in the United Kingdom. Good idea. So how shall we do it? Let's get all single parents (why is it almost always presumed to be single mothers?) into employment. But that is only one sort of poverty. What about the emotional poverty that we are inflicting on children who consequently will have so little of their mother's time? What do we do about them? Provide more nurseries, subsidize the cost of child-minders. Sure, but the proportion of children going into compulsory education who cannot talk well and have extremely limited vocabularies, and are unable to tie their own shoelaces, continues to grow. And so on. Each policy initiative, however good in itself, has unforeseen consequences which give rise to the recognition of another shortcoming. Where does it all end? Of course, it doesn't end; there is no end. There are no short-cuts, no final solutions, and no utopias. Christians know that – or if they do not, they should return to the tradition where they will find their suspicions confirmed. What Christians do know – and the task of the minister flowing from presidency of the celebration of Christ's presence in the sacrament of Holy Communion is to ensure that the community of faith is reminded of it regularly – is that since God *is* present, we have nothing to fear and unlimited resources of love on which to draw.

Pie in the sky when you die? Not a bit of it. Wherever we are, whatever the condition in which we find ourselves, there is always something that we can do to bring about an improvement. And one of the things – perhaps the most important thing – is to remind ourselves of the rock from which we were hewn, to reground ourselves in the tradition, to tell our story and see if we can get going again. Hence the importance of the liturgy.

Liturgy

In ancient Greece a liturgy (*leitourgeia*) was a public service carried out by individuals on behalf of the state at personal expense. It was an honour highly regarded and much preferred (perhaps) to taxation. In the Septuagint it is applied to religious duties; in the Church it has come to be attached to forms of worship in general and the Eucharist in particular. The manner in which I have above developed an understanding of the Eucharist fits this origin, for the Church, in offering itself to God in Christ in the Eucharist, offers a public service on behalf of the world. However, whereas in ancient Greece the qualification for this honour was a certain minimal level of wealth, for the Christian the honour flows simply from the twin fact of a shared humanity and participation in the Body of Christ, the Church. But honour it is – a greater one indeed than comes from the possession of wealth.

The normal pressures of life over the course of the average week, added to those which come from trying to live in the light of faith, gradually undermine one's grasp on the central truths of the Christian life. The consequence is that one needs to be reminded. This process involves joining with the community of faith to link oneself once again with the story of the faith. In worship we remember together the honour that has been bestowed on us by the gift of Christ. Put at its most basic, the outline of our liturgy, of our work together, is as follows.

We first recall together God's presence, recognize our faithlessness, and gather up all our fears and desires in the prayer our Lord taught us – the 'Our Father'. We then listen to the narrative into which we have been introduced, with readings from the Old Testament, the Epistles and the Gospels; the themes arising from them are built into the concerns of the world by the preacher, who shows how they make sense of current anxieties and offer opportunities for further reflection and action. If the liturgy is the Eucharist, we then take up in intercession our concerns for the world and its well-being in the context of our heartfelt gratitude for the gifts we enjoy. This leads to a sharing of God's grace in the distribution of bread and the wine, the body and blood of Christ, and a sending out into the world renewed by God's Spirit to love and serve him.

The natural human search for meaning is grounded and renewed in this celebration: if we have an inkling of what we are doing, we shall be encouraged to get on with the business of living. Not only that, we shall be inspired to pursue the business of making sense of life with all its dimensions, explorations, sensitivities and opportunities, secure in the knowledge that the heart of human experience is rooted in the personal, indestructible, personal being of God.

Ordained ministers are charged with the awful responsibility of bringing their life's experience into relation with the tradition and with the total range of reflection that is open to them. There is then the demanding business of sharing this with others, with all the risks that that entails, with the purpose of exciting others to engage in the enterprise for themselves.

If the minister is to engage with the others in the search for the truth in Christ, there are enormous resources in the many traditions of spiritual reflection on which to draw. It is nothing short of tragic if the minister has not experimented with them and is incapable of drawing on any or all of them in advising others where to go. All of them, from the 'Spiritual Exercises' of Ignatius Loyola, to the extempore prayer of Primitive Methodism and the quiet of Quaker worship, have been found by some on occasions to be just what they needed. I say 'on occasions' because it is pointless to think that there is one style for everybody, or one style for an individual for the whole of his or her life. We are all eclectic. Of course, some ecclesial traditions are closed to some valuable ways, which is why a person's spiritual growth may lead him or her from one tradition to another. The sensitive minister will learn to recognize this and to encourage it. For the person who comes to this conclusion, it will be the result of serious thought and prayer. But when they come to believe that their spiritual life will not be further deepened unless they move into a more congenial ecclesial tradition, they are likely still to be grateful for what they have learned. A spiritual life is a complex trajectory that no minister should want to control: it is in any case impossible. Ministers may, of course, find this true of their own vocation.

Formation

Those who have charge of the preparation of people for ministry have serious work to do: they have extraordinary responsibilities and marvellous opportunities. Those who believe that they may have a vocation need to test it, prove it and grow with it. The testing is one that falls to the Church as a whole, though in the present divided Church the many churches within their own traditions undertake the task. In Methodism the support of both the local circuit and the District Committees are required before examination takes place at a Connexional Committee whose responsibility it is to make a recommendation to the Annual Conference. Conference itself makes the final judgement. The procedure thereafter is controversially complex and demanding because although the training may be said to have begun, further preliminary exploration of the exact nature of the vocation over the course of the following year is required. What form of ministry best suits this person – presbyteral, diaconal or lay, for example? A person may still be advised to withdraw or may choose to withdraw, and for those whom at the end of the year Methodism affirms, there is the question of what educational experience is judged appropriate, if the person is to be equipped to fulfil their calling.

What is clear is that it is not simply up to individuals themselves to determine the situation in their own cases, whatever the strength of their conviction: delusions, ignorance, false expectations and self-deception are too common to be ignored. Certainly too, wider education will be necessary, as well as opportunities for the development of discernment, the capacity to empathise, to listen attentively, and to grow in the love of God. Without knowledge of the tradition, the minister has no ground on which to stand. Without participation in the tradition, the minister has nothing to share. Without awareness of the world, the minister has nothing wherewith to develop understanding. Apart from celebration of the presence of God in Christ in the liturgy, the vision that once lit the minister's way will fade, and without vision the minister will perish through the death of hope.

So formation? Yes, most definitely. But we need to understand what we mean. It concerns a flourishing of the virtues and dispositions that go to make a person real for others. By this, I suggest, formation is a lifetime activity; the process never ends. What is more, it is personal in the sense that ministers have to make the tradition their own. It does mean 'practising the faith' by accepting the discipline of worship and prayer, and the commitment to a moral life focused upon the needs of others and the service of Christ. It means study so as to have the resources on which to base a coherent picture of the world to share with others. It means the development of imagination with which to enliven the vision of what might be. It means a confident willingness to question not simply the implications but the basis of faith, or we shall lose touch with reality. It means the cultivation of a gentle hope in order to have the courage to continue our vocation. It means learning to be one's self with others for the world's sake: which is what we mean when we talk of being Christlike. As Bonhoeffer memorably said, 'Jesus is the man for others.'

Formation can be interpreted so as to justify bullying in order to overlay the real self with a hollow persona of formal appearance. Indeed, the term has meant for some Christian traditions the acceptance of harsh practices in order to break what they regard as the arrogance of the human will and inculcate submission to ecclesiastical authority which they assume to be the will of God. Such a process is in principle a denial of human nature: the consequence has been devastating. Ministers have suffered terribly, leading to personal humiliation, and, on occasions, public disaster for the Church. After all, the real self will not be frustrated; it will out, indeed it cannot be conquered. Liberation, freedom of the human spirit, is always within our grasp; it is precisely what we are promised as members of the Body of Christ. As Christians we are not bound but free. Therefore, properly understood, formation involves a flowering of true human nature, not its neglect or denial. We are not promised that we will be somebody else if we learn to do as we are told, but that we will be ourselves if we will only learn what it is to accept the love of God. But learning what it is to accept the love of God is precisely what we all find so difficult.

A little understanding of psychology may help. At the heart of becoming ourselves and therefore at the heart of the process of formation there must be the recognition that 'there's no such thing as a free love'; even, perhaps especially, in the case of our love of God. Adam Phillips makes this remark in his Master Mind Lecture on Freud which he delivered at the Royal Academy and which is now published in an intriguing book of essays.[1] All love that is given to us is demanding, delightful, seductive, and potentially – but only potentially – life-giving. I say this because it is all too easy to fall into the trap of accepting it at face value and failing to realize that if it is real love, it will require costly work if it is to grow and inspire us with genuine personal nourishment. There are many reasons for this – only three of which can be alluded to here, for reasons of space and for the additional reason that they are complicated and require a complete personal knowledge which none of us possesses. Suffice it to say that they are legion and like the devils; to cast one out is, if one is not careful, simply to create the space for two more!

First, we may be flattered and tempted to believe that we deserve to be loved, whereas, of course, to know that we are loved is first and foremost to be given the freedom to look at ourselves a little more honestly. A person who is loved can afford to do so. Human kind cannot bear too much reality, it is true, but given the love of another, it is possible to bear a little more reality, and, therefore, in the light of deeper self-knowledge, gain the freedom to give a little more of oneself to the other.

Second, there is the very real possibility of giving in to instinctive behaviour and trying to manipulate the other so as to secure one's own ends. This might be interpreted at its most destructive as the illusory search for certainty. If we can fix ourselves in relation to the rest of the world by determining it and its impact on us by putting other people between us and reality, we shall, we might think, have given ourselves ultimate unchallengeable power. We shall confirm ourselves to be in control. But this confirmation is only in our own minds: in fact, of course, we have done no such thing in reality, for we will have lost control of the one thing necessary – ourselves. Therefore the truth is the contrary: in coming to believe that we are in power, we lose authority first over ourselves and then subsequently in the eyes of others. Only by accepting the self-limitation that comes from recognizing the immoveable reality of the other will we flourish. For us, as for all humans, the essence of life is change and growth, and that depends profoundly upon the recognition of the other who is over against us, and a coming to terms with their authority over us, given as it is in the best of circumstances in, with and through love. Indeed it is more than this. For to recognize the authority of the other over us and to accept the other's gift of love is not a matter of passive reception; if personal change and growth are to take place, we shall have first to learn what it is to love ourselves, for on that depends in turn our capacity to master ourselves and give ourselves to the other. That is hard work indeed, for it only comes about when we give honest attention to the power of instinctive desire and the temptation to give in to it.

David would have done well to recognize this when he lusted after Bathsheba and manipulated Uriah into a position where he lost his life. Bathsheba was no doubt desirable in David's eyes; she was, we are told, very beautiful. It may even be true (the story can certainly be read this way) that Bathsheba was flattered by the attention of the king. But since David did not recognize the reality of her otherness, he sought to bring her into his power by intruding into Bathsheba's life and conditioning the world to his advantage. Apparent initial success led to consequences that were disastrous. The outcome of the battle was 'fixed', and her husband Uriah placed in the forefront of the attack so that he was inevitably killed. David must have thought, 'So much for Uriah, now for Bathsheba – she's free!', only to find that the uncomfortable truth will out. He had failed to appreciate the Freudian truth that there is no such thing as a free love, not even a free love when God is the giver. Nathan the prophet brought King David face to face with himself, and he did not like what he saw. Only when he faced up to that was there the opportunity to grow a little in self-knowledge, thereby entering upon his real inheritance and contributing to the realization of God's presence and the foundation of the future kingdom.

Third, to discover that we are loved may suggest that we are cured, whereas it should prompt no more than, and no less than, the even more desirable perception that we are curable. I am using the term 'cure' in a possibly misleading sense. Of course, while there are cures for some conditions – and there are even more that will be curable as medical science, pharmacologists, geneticists and biochemists discover them – there are others that in this limited sense are incurable. In such cases the 'cure' may paradoxically be the willing acceptance of the fact that there is no cure. Then and only then can one face up to oneself in the profound sense to which I am drawing attention here. Notwithstanding all the treatments which have come from the flowering of research over recent decades, in the last resort there is of course no such thing as a cure for death; what there is, is love. St Paul understood this perfectly well, which is why he regarded love (charity) as the ultimate existent. He is right. Apart from its grounding in love and the hard work implied in its acceptance, there is nothing of worth in human experience.

So, formation must be built around these truths of human nature if the persons aspiring to be ministers are to fulfil their potential and enter into the joy of their Lord. It is, after all, built into the tradition – and the tradition must be built into the minister. Christian theology strives to say it with passion and sensitivity. God is free, we say, because God knows God's self utterly. Because God knows God's self, God loves God's self and is therefore single undivided Personhood. In our Christian tradition we express and explore this mystery – mystery because it is so much beyond our own experience, though not beyond our desire or in principle understanding – in the doctrine of the Trinity. One Person exists in the dynamic relationship of Father, Son and Holy Spirit, whose knowledge and love make God free to give God's self utterly and completely to the well-being of the other, namely the creation.

However, as we have seen, there is no such thing as 'a free love', even for God. But marvellously (I use the word advisedly here because it is marvellous in the sense that it could not be expected or required), we have the chance to know and experience the love of God as we share in the faith of all Christians, and join in the conversation of God with the world. This comes about because God is (not was) free to pay the price of love. God has what it takes because God is dependent upon nothing and no one but God's self. God is who God is and not another Being, and will enable us to become ourselves and not other people.

Formation is focused upon the business of enabling the minister who is committed to entering into God's freedom in Christ to give and receive love, and to pay the price. While this remains a voluntary decision, and a voluntary activity, it will have the potential to free the minister to grow into and share the life of 'the man for others'. It cannot be emphasized too strongly or too frequently that this is a lifetime experience: ordination is for life and is a mark on the soul.

There are implications for the content of the curriculum and the nature of the pedagogy that should be offered to any person seeking to enter into ministry. Let's look first at pedagogy, because unless that is right, there will be little of worth communicated in the 'facts' passed on in the curriculum. Those involved in delivering the curriculum will need to do so as scholars who are inviting their students to join them in their own search for the truth. 'Let's have a look at this' should be the approach, not 'Take this down and commit it to memory.' There should, of course, be plenty of actual 'remembering', but to the extent that teaching and learning are not regarded as mutual exploration it will betray the very nature of the relationships into which we want to draw the student.

Socrates, it appears, was accustomed to take his students for a walk round the stoa, engaging them in vigorous conversation. By this he made them realize for themselves where they stood on various critical matters, and what the underlying assumptions were on which their opinions were based. In this way they become responsible for their own learning and thus better students. Our pedagogy must share some of the same characteristics. We are looking to engage people in the continuing conversation that God initiated in creation, not ciphers or poodles, noisy gongs or clanging cymbals. It is no soft option for the teachers involved, for the doubts which we have as teachers will be brought out with all the attendant risks of criticism, rejection and suspicion. There will be little of which we can be certain, because there is little that is certain. But of one thing we can be certain: we are introducing ministers to matters that are of ultimate significance. We are helping them to begin to study, to think and feel in ways that will open their minds and refresh their spirits, with the result that they will be able to bear the pain of trying to do the same for others. It cannot be emphasized too often: this is something which is beginning and which will never end. One may rest from time to time; perhaps one should. But in this particular war, there is no peace.

An essential ingredient of the curriculum will be the Bible, but it will be vital to get across right at the beginning just what sort of material the Bible contains. It is above all, a living conversation, drawing on material from 1,000 years of Jewish and Christian history, which is developed out of the curiosity of countless previous generations. Like most conversations, it is diverse, written in many styles by a wide range of participants, reflecting many moods, sometimes incoherent, frequently puzzling, always focused on the task of coming to terms with the nature, reality and being of God and God's relationship with the world. In the conventional way in which one talks of these things, the Bible contains truth, it does not state the Truth; the Bible points to God's loving presence, it does not embody it in leather covers; the Bible should be discussed, critically analysed, reflected upon, questioned, put in context and vigorously argued with. Only then can we hope to be successful in our attempts to 'read, learn and inwardly digest' it.

It would be invidious to go through an adequate curriculum since, as with the National Curriculum, no sooner has one put together a decent stab at concocting one, than three other matters are raised. So we need knowledge of history – and not just what is called ecclesiastical history. Properly understood, for example (*pace* Oscar Cullmann), salvation history (*Heilsgeschichte*) includes every aspect of human experience understood in terms of the relationship of the creator with the creation – and there's no time for all that. This underlines the importance of the approach that is taken rather than the period of history that is attended to. From the point of view of Methodism, we need to take seriously the early centuries of the Church and the catholic tradition, as well as the Reformation and the eighteenth-century revival since, but for the catholic tradition, the bug of the early Church fathers on which Methodism stands would not have bitten Wesley.

And science? Yes, indeed, in the very broadest sense, both physical and social. These should be drawn on because they represent in their many ways the developing human response to the world of God's creation.

Their success testifies to the God-given capacity to furnish the human mind with the stimulating opportunity to understand the world and to apply the implications of the knowledge thus gained in affectionate partnership with God's redemptive creativity. Again, it will be the manner in which the various insights of the many scientific disciplines are discussed that will be significant, as much as their content. It will be essential, above all, to follow truth wherever it leads, not to fear it.

Theology should become the bread of life to the minister. How else are the experience of a lifetime, the imaginative explorations of the arts, the considered judgements of the sciences, the analytical modelling of mathematics and the ordered arguments of the philosophers to be held together? Theology may no longer be regarded as the queen of the sciences, but for the Christian its energy, revelatory power and ambitious aspiration are of the essence of what it is to be human. We want to know, and we believe that in Christ through the work of the Holy Spirit, we shall be encouraged to go on finding out.

There is for all Churches a Magisterium, by which we mean authoritative teaching which is the produce of centuries of enquiry, definition and reflection. The historical Creeds constitute its briefest statement: the sacraments are celebrations of it: the decisions of the Ecumenical Councils claim to determine some of it. The Roman Catholic Church has the most refined and developed version of it. However, there is across the Church universal no agreement on the exact form of the creeds, which creeds are included, which Councils are recognized, or who has the authority to develop and grow it. In an important sense (almost) all Churches accept that God has yet more light and truth to share with the human world of enquiry and faith. Certainly the Methodist Church does. In the simplest sense Methodism might be said to be open to new insights from all directions and is not prejudiced about the people or places to whom or in which new truth may break in. The judgement regarding a proposed 'new direction' will be made by a body, the Conference, made up of both lay and ordained persons, after consideration through the local courts of circuit meeting and District Synods, likewise comprised of lay and ordained persons. Hence the formation of a minister has to take account of the importance of responding to the prompting of the Spirit to recognize truth when it is intuited, discovered and debated.

But I return to the essential matter of self-knowledge. Do we take that with sufficient seriousness? I doubt it. There is either an intrusive demand to 'spill the beans', or an awful standing back from deep engagement because of the mistaken assumption that personal knowledge is necessarily private and 'off limits'. Both views are based on a misunderstanding and owe nothing to the Christian tradition. The demand to 'spill the beans' about oneself to another as if he or she had a right to know is outrageous. Not even God makes that sort of demand. God's giving of God's self to us enables us to see that we are free to share a bit more of ourselves with God. Only if we attempt to bring potential ministers to see their own freedom in relation to God's love will they become free to grow in faith. On the other hand, to stand back as if each person can find his or her own way unaided is likewise to fail the tradition. By engaging people in conversation with God, we shall help them to find themselves and be freed to free others.

Dare we do this? I hope so. If we do not, the Church will become an irrelevant set of automata, not the body of affectionate heroes inspired to love the world in the name of God.

Pastoral care

This chapter informs our understanding of pastoral care, which is how we express our love of the world when it is informed by participation in the Church's conversation with Christ on behalf of the world. Pastoral care concerns all aspects of life as we know it, all creation and all humankind. It is not aggressive or power-seeking, but, if we get it right, it will be authoritative because it offers the liberty of the love of God, promises the hope of wisdom, carries conviction and points to God, Father, Son and Holy Spirit, in whom all things live and move and have their being. Of course, for ministers, as for all other people, love begins with oneself, for if one does not love oneself, one lacks the freedom to love others. The reason for this is simple: if one does not love oneself, one has not yet accepted the love of God in Christ, without which there is neither freedom nor truth. What we offer in an apparently barren and spare universe, bereft of human character, is the food of eternal life. That is our living tradition.

Bread

Hunger was loneliness, betrayed
By the pitiless candour of the stars'
Talk, in an old byre he prayed

Not for food; to pray was to know
Waking from a dark dream to find

The white loaf on the white snow;
Not for warmth, warmth brought the rain's
Blurring of the essential point
Of ice probing his raw pain.

He prayed for love, love that would share
His rags' secret; rising he broke
Like sun crumbling the gold air

The live bread for the starved folk.

R. S. Thomas[2]

Notes

1 Adam Phillips, *Side Effects*, London: Penguin, 2006, p. 6.
2 *Poetry for Supper,* London: Rupert Hart-Davis, 1958, p. 46; R. S. Thomas, *The Collected Poems 1945–1990*, London, J. M. Dent, 1993, p. 93.

6

Ministry, Spirituality and Strategy

MARK WAKELIN

Why ministers should read this chapter

We cannot choose whether we manage people or not. If we work with others and have some sort of responsibility for what they do, we are 'in management'. The question is, 'Do we manage well or badly?' More exactly, do we manage in a way that makes sense of our calling to ministry and the graciousness of God's gift, the Church?

This chapter is an invitation to consider the potential and possibilities for ministry when ministers engage with two things at once: thinking strategically and reflecting theologically. In it, I do not offer a comprehensive introduction to either theological reflection or strategic thinking, but rather an encouragement to think, and to keep thinking in both spheres of knowledge. People in ministry come to it with a wide range of secular experiences that they bring to their work; they also have a good grounding in theological thinking. The challenge here is to do the two things at the same time: to ask strategic questions of a theological reality; the Church; and to ask theological questions of strategic approaches to an organization. I make the invitation because I simply believe that the Church needs something of the clear thinking, honesty, courage and challenge of a more strategic approach to its ministry, and that we can only do that with integrity if we keep our Christian hats on and allow our theological understanding to inform that approach.

For a number of years now I have run training programmes with titles such as 'Theology and Strategy' and 'Thinking Systematically and Reflecting Theologically'. A part of me has wondered if anyone would be interested. Theology is frequently looked upon as at best dull and at worst corrupting, and strategy as just 'management speak' that has no place in the Church. What has constantly impressed me, however, is the keenness that people do bring to both these areas, and I have learned a great deal from them. This approach really seems to help people in their ministry.

My own view is that the Church can make two major mistakes about the theories, competencies, procedures and practices that contribute to modern organizational theory and management: they can either ignore them totally and claim that because the Church is far more than simply an organization, organizational theories should not apply; or they can believe that the Church is just another organization and we can apply any theory or practice we like, confident in the knowledge that such 'technologies' are ethically and philosophically neutral. The first seems plain daft; if nothing else, the Church is an organization, and the more we can understand it as such, the more likely we are to be useful in our ministry. The second is simply dangerous; the Church is also a miracle, and plastering over it some secular approach without due care can obscure what it is about.

A last word by way of introduction: what makes this approach valid isn't whether or not others have found it useful, or whether you can read about it in academic books, but quite simply: does it help in thinking through an approach to ministry? The only real way to make sense of the ideas is to try them out before you have decided if they are any good. To do this requires a limited amount of trust in the author, and a great deal of faith in your own judgement and capacity to play with an idea and decide on its merit. If it helps you to trust me, then all I can say is that I've been trying to think strategically and reflect theologically for many years, as a circuit minister, as National Secretary of the Methodist Association of Youth Clubs, as Director of the Guy Chester Centre and as a trainer and consultant with a variety of organizations – Anglican and Methodist, Roman Catholic and Baptist, from the YMCA to Methodist Superintendents, from the Carmelite Community to Christian Aid gap-year students.

The language of strategy

As Lindbeck[1] and others have demonstrated, the language and grammar of a discipline not only enables the subject to be communicated but also shapes and informs its practice. What is true of theology is just as true of practical pastoral ministry and of strategic church management. I have therefore called this section 'The language of strategy' because learning to minister strategically and theologically entails learning a new language and developing the confidence necessary to communicate using it. Taking the time to learn this language is important, not least because it forms an important and useful part of the process of team building and hence of ministry. Ministers are not separate from their congregations, and cannot effectively 'communicate' the gospel without the support of others. When ministers lack the language to communicate their vision and the necessary strategies for implementing it, then it can be frustrating for them and the Church: ministry can break down and the relationship between the minister and the Church becomes severely tested.

It is important to note from the onset, however, that although many of the words associated with management strategies may sound familiar, they are in fact used in many different ways by different people. On the one hand, this doesn't matter; words are flexible enough! On the other hand, learning and agreeing to use at least some words in the same way is essential if a leadership team is to communicate effectively. Scholes and Johnson,[2] for example, have no final authority which allows them to claim 'Our way of defining a "vision" is right and everyone else wrong'; it is simply useful to agree at the outset of a strategic review that we all mean the same thing by the word.[3] In building a team, it can, of course, be just as important to learn how not to use technical or strategic language on certain occasions. The task of translating strategic or theological language into less 'technical' terms, however, demands a fairly precise and confident grasp of the language of both in the first place. Thus the task of learning the language really is indispensible. This is a familiar task for ministers who, through their training, have already had to acquire the 'language skills' necessary to enable them to manage the learning of a congregation through their weekly translation of the Word into words, whether spoken in the sermon or rehearsed in the liturgy.

Although not intended as a survey or summary of organizational theory, the following example drawing on the language and approach to strategic thinking found in standard Master of Business Administration (MBA) course book about corporate organization will help to illustrate the approach to ministry that I am advocating.[4]

Vision is an overriding statement of purpose. A vision is inspirational, a guiding star, something that may be outside an individual's or organization's capacity to bring about. It is unchanging, challenging and essential.

Mission is a clear statement of where individuals or organizations are within that vision. The mission statement is a narrowing of the vision; it is obtainable, possible and realistic. It is what people or organizations are about now, who they are now; their part in the overall scheme of things for the present. Mission and vision go together and are often confused. A vision statement can be recognized because the question 'Why?' cannot be asked of it. It is the top of the hierarchy of ideas. Vision does not change and is not usually obtainable in the lifetime of the person or organization.

On the other hand, a mission can be accomplished, though sometimes with difficulty, and it can change, although rarely.

Goals are broadly the things that must be achieved if the mission is to be fulfilled. They are something to aim for. They are also choices; there may be other goals that would help in achieving the mission, but these are the ones chosen for now. It often helps to notice what has not been chosen in order to be clearer about what has been chosen and why.

Objectives are clearly described, time-lined, specific, measurable expressions of the goals. Organizations find objectives very hard to write, and I will come back to setting well-formed goals and objectives later. If the objectives are not right, everything else is harder to do. Goals and objectives are often confused. It is important, however, that what is aimed for is understood in increasingly clear and specific terms. It should be possible to ask questions like: 'What would it look like if we succeeded?', 'How is it possible to know if what was intended was in fact achieved?' There are some very interesting questions, explored later, about what this means for Church and ministry where quantifiable outcomes don't necessarily define success; but it is precisely when you get such interesting questions that the language of strategy really gets exciting!

Strategies are the broad brush-stroke approaches that are chosen to achieve specific objectives; where the resources of time, money, skills and effort are allocated. They are descriptions of the kind of work that will be done; a strategic approach is by definition a quickly described one. It is a conceptual approach to problem-solving and even large organizations can establish their strategic plan in a short time. The more detailed work occurs in being clear about the objectives and in clearly identifying the mission (see above) and in determining the projects and tasks that need to be done (see below).

Tasks are the various actions or projects that will fulfil a strategy. This is where the detailed planning work takes place, where the allocation of resources begins to take a much firmer shape. Budgets allocated through creating strategy are spent in determining tasks! Tasks, like objectives, are time-lined and it is possible to be specific about the resources that are allocated to them.

Control is the process by which the effectiveness of tasks is monitored and evaluated. It answers the question of how to determine whether various projects are achieving what it is hoped they would achieve. Control becomes possible if objectives are sufficiently specific, and impossible otherwise. Control involves the monitoring and evaluating of outcomes. The measure is both against what it had been hoped would be achieved (objectives) and the real reasons behind the endeavours (the vision and mission). Attempting to monitor and evaluate achievements that are not easily quantifiable is clearly problematic. This is a concern, as most of the things that ministry seeks to achieve are not quantifiable in any empirical or 'meaningful' sense. However, 'difficult' isn't the same as 'impossible', and it is not the case that 'because what a minister does is not easily measurable, there is no point in this process'!

Reward is the response made when what was set out as something to be achieved, was achieved. In a commercial organization it may be expressed in financial rewards, promotion, or some form of public acknowledgement. It provides the opportunity to 'think through the shot' as golfers say; that is, think through all the challenges of the work to a successful conclusion. This in itself is both motivating and idea generating, but it also allows all the people in the organization who have been part of the vision in the first place to be properly valued.

Reflecting upwards and downwards

Each level of strategic thinking requires choices to be made. This strategy is chosen rather than that one; this is the mission and not something else. Choices are made within the genuine possibilities that are on offer; they are made between real alternatives. This is important, as not choosing, or choosing something that is too broad and inclusive (which amounts to the same thing), risks dissipating energy. Ill-thought-through church mission statements, for example, often do more harm than good because they burden a congregation with an impossible mission that is so ill defined that it neither motivates people to act nor helps them to prioritize the use of their resources. The 'failure' of a minister to either manage or 'deliver' on an ill-thought-through church mission has been known to provoke a crisis of vocation for many in ministry. It is undoubtedly a contributory cause to the increasing number of those who leave the ministry within the first five years. Being able to identify a good from a bad mission statement is thus essential, and this in turn is dependent on being able to make the right choices in the strategic thinking process.

Every strategic choice prompts the question, 'According to what criteria?', or 'How are these choices made?' This can be answered by reflecting upwards towards the vision, 'Is this choice in line with the vision?', and downwards to control, 'Does this strategy work?' Both are needed. Although ministers are increasingly familiar with the concept of the Pastoral Cycle[5] and the need to develop reflective practices, there is still a tendency to separate out 'church management' from ministerial practice as though church management is somehow unrelated to the work of the gospel or the vision of the kingdom. The next section therefore provides a simple worked example followed by a more concrete illustration of how strategic thinking can be applied to ministerial practice.

A worked example

Scholes and Johnson give an example of how this kind of thinking can be applied to a personal intention.[6] I have worked with it myself to include a more theological rationale!

Vision – to give glory to God by being 'full alive'.

Mission – to be healthier.

Goals – to lose weight and get fitter.

Objectives – to lose ten pounds by Christmas and run four miles in 40 minutes.

Strategy – diet and exercise.

Tasks – reduce calories in a day to 1,800, exercise four times a week for 40 minutes.

Control – weigh myself before breakfast every Monday morning, keep a running log of my distances and times.

Reward – buy a new suit.

This simple example illustrates the key principles involved in the process of strategic thinking. First notice choice: I choose a *vision* that inspires me, that makes sense of everything I do, and gives me a reason to want to keep going. This vision is compelling and for me true. It matters. I choose a *mission* that fits the vision, but is far narrower. I could choose other missions – for example, I could choose something about relationships. I may indeed want to tackle this as well, but to do so would divert my resources and attention and I would have to make the judgement as to whether this was possible. I might like to choose this mission for a period of time and then return and ask, 'What other missions might I undertake to fulfil my vision?'

I choose these *goals* and not others. I could, for example, have chosen to develop a better prayer life (spiritual health) rather than get physically healthier. There is nothing wrong with this choice; it might indeed be the better choice. I may have good reason, however, for the choice I made. My physical health may be a priority for me, and while I will need to come back to my spiritual health in the very near future, I need to get a grip on something that is undermining the whole of my well-being. I may, indeed, decide I need two goals, one reflecting a spiritual concern and the other a physical one; but to do so I need to ask, 'Have I the resources of time and energy to do both at once, or does one have a priority for me?'

I choose these *objectives* because I believe that they are possible; I think ahead to the idea of control and say, 'Is it possible to lose so much weight by Christmas?', 'Do I have it in me to run a mile every ten minutes for 40 minutes?' I choose them because they accord with my vision and mission: 'Is this weight loss essentially a healthy amount?', 'Do these objectives in any way give glory to God?'. It is not difficult to imagine choices of objectives that might make me unhealthy or indeed make God very unhappy indeed. I could, for example, choose to aim at unhealthy amounts of weight loss, or dangerous amounts of exercise.

I choose these *strategies* because I believe they will be effective in achieving my goals and objectives and because I think they will essentially make me healthier and thus 'give God glory'.

I choose these *tasks* for the same 'upwards and downwards' reasons. I believe they will work in achieving my objectives, and I believe they contribute not only to my objectives but to my vision and mission, to be healthier and to give God glory by being fully alive. The old joke about diet, 'How do you lose ten pounds of ugly flesh in a single stroke?' 'Cut off you head', makes the point. Achieving your objectives is never enough. You need to achieve objectives that are still linked to your vision and mission, otherwise it's pointless! The number of calories I decide I need to consume is determined by knowledge I have of what constitutes a healthy amount for a man who wants to lose weight to eat. I might want to expand this description to take into account what constitutes a balanced diet. In choosing both the tasks and strategies it is important to note that external advice may be needed if I am to fulfil both my vision/mission statements and my intended goals/objectives.

I choose this method of *control* because it too is consistent with both effectiveness and vision. As any one who has gone on a diet will know, the temptation to weigh too often, or even to avoid weighing yourself altogether, is high. To do so in a controlled and wise way is more effective; I'm more likely to achieve my objectives and stay in line with my vision/ mission, which is about health and glory rather than obsession or denial!

I choose a way to *reward* myself that will genuinely motivate me, is effective, and is true to my vision/mission. For example, it is tempting on a diet to reward yourself by climbing into the fridge, closing the door, and eating mayonnaise with a serving spoon. If you have never wanted to do this, you have either never been on a diet, or you simply prefer chocolate spread. Buying a suit is not dead centre to either my vision or my mission – it might, for example, be pandering to simple vanity, which is detrimental to my health and not particularly glorifying to God; however, it might also simply make me feel really good and confident and transform my Sunday preaching! The way the choice of reward is made is the same as every other choice: 'Is it effective?' and 'Does it make sense of my vision/mission?'

The application of strategic thinking to ministry: a process of disentangling

Most ministers' first attempts at strategic thinking either with, or on behalf of, their churches invariably lead to them being 'tangled up' in the process. This is not surprising. The process of strategic thinking, however, is essentially about 'untangling'; something that is always difficult to do but which can be learned. Moreover, it is the actual process of untangling that makes strategic thinking so formative and valuable. It can be both revelatory and transformative.

'My vision is for house groups in my church'

I remember a minister who had a 'real vision for house groups' in his local church. It was compelling and passionate, but he found that his vision was tangled and difficult to share and communicate, and he couldn't see what options he had, or even express clearly why he felt that this vision mattered so much to him. The process of untangling his vision not only gave him ways to communicate and share his hopes for the church, but also helped him motivate his congregation, and above all to understand the real choices he had before him. Thinking of house groups as the vision is understandable because 'vision' is used in the sense of 'I can imagine and see the church with house groups.' In fact it can really help to conceptualize goals and objectives in very visual ways. However, in working with this particular use of language, it is clear that a house group isn't itself the vision. How can we know this? Basically because you can ask, 'Does it have a purpose?' As it isn't an end itself, it isn't the vision. Recognizing this can be important as it prompts the person to look for and discover the vision that lies behind this idea. In finding that vision the person will first of all find something motivational, second will find something unifying, and third will find something that makes it possible to see the choices that are implicit in the real vision.

To continue with the example, a house group could be one of a number of things in the language of strategy. It could be a goal or an objective, for example, but it would probably be more helpful to think of it as a *strategy*: a way of achieving something in broad brush-stroke terms; for example, a particular approach to discipleship, Christian nurture and education, pastoral care and fellowship. House groups are useful things, but they are not ends in themselves. It is possible to ask, 'What purpose do they have?' Asking this creates the opportunity to uncover the objectives, goals, mission and vision that lie behind house groups. We may, for example, determine that a house group's highest purpose is 'to give glory to God'. Knowing this will affect everything; it is why knowing the vision matters so much.

If the vision is known, then the chosen mission can be stated in language that both affirms the vision, 'It is in this way and by being this kind of people that we will glorify God', and suggests goals and objectives, 'We need to achieve the following things if we are to be this kind of people.' For example, it may be decided that the mission behind the intention to start house groups is to 'bring people closer to God and each other'. This knowledge leads to the realization that what is needed are goals and objectives that will clarify what is meant by the term 'people who are closer to God'. Notice the potentially theologically rich nature of goals and objectives.

Ministers often get stuck at this point. They either feel that such goals are impossible to identify and so avoid making any kind of goal at all, or they decide on some other simpler goal or objective that is easier to define such as 'numbers of people'. The qualitative research community has a saying, 'If you can count it, that ain't it', which is a fair description of the challenge facing ministers who want to set clear objectives. We need to keep asking, 'What does success look like?' If we discover the real vision that lies behind so many of the more ordinary intentions of ministry, it may well be possible to ask, 'What does the kingdom look like?' That is a very rich vein of both theological reflection and strategic thinking.

I asked the person who had a vision for house groups, 'What would the church look like if you succeeded?' To answer that question is not only to find the most profound forms of motivation, but also to open up a creative seam of choices and complementary ideas. Setting goals and objectives means finding increasingly detailed and specific descriptions of what success will look like. Numbers may well form part of those descriptions, for example in response to the questions concerning 'How many people?' and what 'being closer to God and each other' really means in the context of this particular mission. I want to return to this most interesting of questions later; it is at the heart of leadership to ask, 'What does a church look like where people are growing as disciples?'

'My main strategy is to improve our worship'

It sometimes happens that people confuse something far more important with a strategy. Worship is too fundamentally part of our understanding of what it is to be human to be relegated to a 'means to an end', a way of 'bringing people in'. It is understandable why we might see it in these terms. Worship that leads us into the throne room of grace, that leaves us 'lost in wonder, love and praise', is profoundly compelling. However, worship is not a strategy, it is not a means of filling a church. If ever it does become a strategic device for church growth, then its essential purpose is lost. In a similar way there are churches which view friendship as a conversion strategy. The 'stranger in the midst' is befriended in order that they might be persuaded to become a Christian. Friendship, like worship, however, belongs higher in the hierarchy of ideas that forms a strategic plan. To place worship, friendship, fellowship, or even 'signs and wonders' as simply strategies is profoundly corrupting for the Church: gifts of God reduced to marketing tools. It is possible, even desirable, to look to identify strategies that may help in the development of friendships, improvements to our worship and which encourage deeper fellowship; but to see something so precious as simply a means to 'get them into the church' undermines the values and vision of all Christian ministry. How demoralizing it must be to know that the reason you were befriended was to market the Christian religion! How dreadful that in a consumer society, worship might be designed as PR, a front window to entice people in.

Why discovering our vision matters

Visionary leadership is often requested by Churches without any clear idea as to what is meant by the term. The first step in releasing the potential for visionary leadership is engaging in a process which enables vision to be recognized and prioritized. Vision matters because it unites, it motivates, it offers a measure for our efforts and it creates the opportunities for other choices to be opened up. It is surprising how many ordinary ministerial and church habits and practices have a higher intention behind them. It may not always be articulated, but it is invariably there. Even bad habits can have, and probably do have, higher intentions.

I sometimes do an exercise called 'chunking'* which is a way of making explicit something that already exists in our unconscious. Chunking refers to the process of going up and down a hierarchy of ideas with the sort of questions identified earlier, such as 'For what purpose?' The process of making explicit what is tacit, of bringing into the conscious mind what is unconscious, is a powerful way of coming to understand something of our own deepest longings and desires. In ministerial practice and formation, it helps to locate and clarify the sense of vision that actually lies behind so much seemingly mundane, churchy practice. It takes time and practice, but if the question 'For what purpose?' is repeatedly asked of even simple intentions such as tidying the vestry, it soon becomes evident how the task is linked to some profound intentions of ministry and serving God. These links are important; not only are they the reason for doing something in the first place, they also provide the motivation for it.

Vision unifies because while people may not agree on a particular strategy such as 'start house groups', they will almost always agree with the vision 'give glory to God' or 'deepen our Christian fellowship'. This is surprisingly important in meetings. If the purpose behind a particular proposal can be agreed on, it can engender a strong sense of unity. The disagreement about how to implement that vision is often correspondingly less heated.

Vision motivates because people are more likely to become involved with something once they understand the intentions that lie behind it. You can put your own management story in here, but I like the one about the man at NASA who was sweeping the floor. When asked by a visiting politician what he was doing, he answered, 'I'm putting a person on the moon.' Knowing the higher purpose of any mundane task is highly motivating.

A clearly stated vision also offers a measure for each endeavour, because at each level of the hierarchy of ideas the question can be asked, 'Is it in line with our vision?' Vision increases the number of available choices for ministry because, having identified the higher intention behind a fairly basic proposal, it then becomes possible to ask, 'What else will

---

* 'Chunking' and 'higher intentions' are both expressions used in Neuro Linguistic Programming (NLP). NLP is not really a coherent approach to anything in particular, but is an eclectic set of tools to uncover and affect one's unconscious. The idea of going upwards and downwards in the hierarchy of ideas is called 'chunking' and it is a deliberate attempt to avoid very cerebral answers by encouraging someone to articulate their unconscious assumptions. My own training in this was with WestOne, who run a number of training courses in NLP at the Guy Chester Centre.

achieve that?' This may engender complementary ideas, alternative ideas or process ideas. Complementary ideas complement what was originally decided. So 'giving glory to God' as the vision behind the proposal to start house groups prompts the question, 'What else are we going to do that will give God glory?' Alternative ideas may well help with the people who object to the proposal, 'If not house groups, what else can we do?' Process ideas are about the 'how' of the doing – 'We can't start any old house groups, but only ones that give glory to God.'

Clarifying goals and objectives

The process of refining objectives from goals matters. It is a process as much as anything else, a willingness to keep thinking and imagining what should happen. Three things lie at the heart of the clarifying process. The first is effort; it is all too easy to stop thinking because thinking takes effort. It takes effort and energy for the minister to repeatedly ask of themselves and of the Church leadership group, 'What is it that we really want to happen?' The desire to 'just get on with it' is sometimes overwhelming. What does it matter if the leadership team has only the vaguest idea of what they hope will happen? The harsh reality of organizational life, however, is that the more often that nothing in particular is aimed at, the more likely it is that nothing in particular will be hit! The second is honesty; it is all too easy also to remain in fantasy about the reality of a situation. This can either be a fantasy of despair ('Nothing is possible, there are no solutions to the problem or situation'), or it can be the fantasy of blind optimism ('Things really aren't that bad'), and all that is needed is to just keep reassuring ourselves that with a fair wind behind us we will survive. Honesty requires us to look the situation in the face and then reflect on the possibilities in hope.

As Moltmann has conclusively demonstrated, hope is a very different category of mode from optimism, and is an important part of Christian leadership.[7] Doubts are fine; we all have them, and faith is our response. Despair, though, is a fundamental sin; I don't mean the despair of depression and illness, but the intellectual despair of cynicism and world-weariness. Optimism looks at the glass that is half empty and comforts itself with the belief that it is half full. Hope looks at the same glass, and in the light of the promises of God sees the glass full and running over.

To bring effort and honesty to bear upon the task of setting realistic and hopeful goals and objectives, a third factor is needed, and that is courage. Leadership is about courage – the courage to be honest, the courage to try things out, and above all the courage to make mistakes. As a circuit minister, I had some training responsibilities for other churches, and I used to ask a question of leadership teams, 'When did you last fail?' The answer was nearly always, 'We can't remember.' Failure was not part of their story as a church. Of course this wasn't true in an absolute sense, for no organization is perfectly run! However, it was true for them. They had simply never had any goals and objectives clear enough to be able to discern failure. These three things – effort, honesty and courage – form the basis of Scott Peck's solution to procrastination.[8] Together, he says, they amount to love, and it seems that love is at the heart of our hope and faith, of our belief in God, and what God can do with honest, brave people who are prepared to make an effort.

The secret of grasping nettles

A great deal of leadership is about the courage required to grasp nettles, and I was once told the secret by an old Norfolk gardener. His ability to pick up nettles with his bare hands fascinated me as I watched him as a child. 'How do you do that?' I'd ask, truly impressed. He would show me, and with his worn, calloused hands he would gently stroke the nettle upwards and lift it from the ground. I tried it. It hurt. It always hurt, but I knew somehow that there was a secret, if only I could keep on trying. Over the years I have kept having a go to see if I could repeat this gardener's feat of grasping nettles. It hurt every time. As I look back on my gardening career, I have slowly come to realize what his secret was. There is no magic. His calloused hands may have blunted the sting a little, his gentle stroking upwards with the grain of the little needles that deliver the pain so effectively may have minimized their impact, but the real secret is to accept that it will hurt, but get on with it. Nettles won't kill you, they just hurt and the hurt will end. I have avoided so much pain in my ministry that it would have been better had I endured, not raised issues that needing raising, avoiding conflicts, avoiding people even. I have avoided the pain of failure by avoiding thinking through what it was I wanted to achieve, when all that was really needed was the ability to grasp the nettle – the effort, courage and honesty that constitute love.

Outcomes, inputs and outputs

One of the most important distinctions that has to be made in strategic thinking is between outcomes, inputs and outputs. Inputs are the resources that are put into the work. Outputs are what is done with those resources. Outcomes are the consequences of both. It is much easier to measure inputs and outputs than outcomes, so that is what most people tend to do. Governments, for example, regardless of their political persuasion, try to convince others of their successes by narrating how impressive their inputs or outputs are. They might say, for example, that they have put a billion pounds into the National Health Service. This is an input, it reflects their priorities a little, and they could have put the money into something else, or indeed simply not taxed us as much. It doesn't say very much, however, about the NHS. They might say instead, 'We have built ten new hospitals and employed 1,000 extra nursing staff.' This is an output; again this says something about how they have used the resources, but it still doesn't tell people what they really want to know. Surprisingly, the NHS doesn't exist to either spend billions of pounds or to build hundreds of hospitals; these are merely some of the things it does in order to achieve something more important. It is this 'more important' something that is the hoped-for out-come. What is the outcome of all that extra money and all those new hos-pitals and increased staffing levels? The hoped-for outcome should be something to do with health – a healthier nation, for example. In order to measure the success or otherwise of all that spending and effort, the government needs to determine how effective it has been in achieving the outcomes that it intended in the first place. Are we healthier as a nation? Measuring outcomes is the most important thing that can be done, because intended outcomes are the only things that can truly demonstrate the effectiveness of the chosen strategies.

Ministers, just like everyone else, are prone to measure their success by inputs and outputs. They might, for example, aim to have a youth club. After all their hard work they will tell themselves that they have done well in establishing one, recruiting and training the leaders, equipping it, and persuading the PCC that it is going to be well managed and worthwhile. But all these matters are only the inputs and outputs, the resources that have been identified and the use that they have been put to. The real question that the minister should have asked is, 'What were the intended outcomes of the youth club?' When the decision was taken to start a youth club, what was the higher purpose behind it? What would it be like if we achieved *that* purpose?

It is more pertinent to ask the question, 'What does success look like, what might be reasonably expected from our youth club?' The more often ministers learn to ask this question, the better; the deeper they are prepared to delve into their own answers, the more spiritually aware they will be of the theological nature of their decisions and of what they are asking of themselves and of the Churches. This in turn increases the opportunity of achieving something that they too are able to recognize as being 'worthwhile' and hence lessens the likelihood of 'failure' in ministry and crisis of vocation.

The problem is that there is little in existing ministerial training which encourages ministers to probe their motives until they are able to see past the 'desired outcomes'. In the above illustration, for example, some may answer, 'Because we want more young people to come to church' – this is what the minister repeatedly hears from the PCC. Yet youth workers, quite understandably, blanch at this as a motive, preferring to talk instead of wanting to serve young people wholly on their own terms. But before the initial answer is completely dismissed out of hand, it is worth digging deeper to discover why the Church wants young people to attend. Granted, there are all kinds of reasons, some less altruistic than others. Nonetheless, it is likely that behind the simple, 'We want more young people to come to church', lies a higher intention that is linked in some way to the belief that Church is about new life, healing, hope and fulfilment.

If ministers can begin to practise the sort of strategic thinking that prompts them to seek their 'higher intentions', then not only will they bring to the fore their theological as well as sociological thinking, but, as was noted earlier, they will be more likely to empower the Church that they serve to recognize the value of the project. Vision, as was noted earlier, unites, motivates and gives choices. If the purpose of the youth club is expressed in terms of the higher intentions of the project, then youth workers and most church members might agree about the important things! It could, for example, be expressed by the statement 'Young people growing and developing as God wants them to.' Although people might still disagree about the role that 'coming to church' plays in that intention, they can at least begin to glimpse the direction of the youth work. That in turn provides a different answer to the question, 'What are the intended outcomes for our youth work?' The answer is now more likely to be in terms of young people growing and developing as God intends. If this is the intended outcome, it will shape the way in which the whole project is approached.

Staying with the idea of a youth club as 'a good thing in itself' may still have allowed the minister to get away with setting up and running any old youth club, and as long as it was filled and the church was still standing on the Sunday, no one would be bothered. But if the intended outcome is recognized as being to 'help young people grow and develop as God intends', then the minister is prompted to engage with the theologically rich, complex but very interesting question, 'How does God want young people to develop and grow?' This enables them to invite the church to consider the wider question, 'How can our youth club help us achieve this intended outcome?', and to ponder on the vision prompted by the question, 'What would it look like if young people in the church were growing and developing as God intends?'

Well-formed objectives

The most interesting question in all this is to identify what ministerial objectives or outcomes really are. I have expressed this question in a number of ways above, and I want to explore these questions now in more detail. I have found that we all find this question hard.

Most ministers blanch at the question, 'What does success look like?' for a wide variety of reasons. In the first place, Christian ministers struggle with the idea of success in any form. 'We aren't meant to be successful, just faithful', is often said. This is understandable; at the heart of the faith is Christ crucified, the opposite of worldly success. But who said anything about the intended success being 'worldly'? Is it not possible to keep following the crucified and risen Christ and subvert the whole concept of success? It is also, quite accurately, said, 'You can't measure ministerial success.' Of course not, but it is possible to make a judgement about it based on ordinary human observation and reflection, and upon divine inspiration and prayer. This is where the whole business of theological reflection and strategic thinking gets really exciting. It is precisely at the point of asking, 'What does ministerial success look like?' that the tough, honest, brave and helpful questions of strategic thinking come up against the inspiring, challenging, world-changing concepts of Christ-centred ministry and theology. The main objection is that it is simply hard to determine our goals, and the only answer to this is, 'Of course it is, that is why we need Christian leadership!'

One of the key measurements of church success is usually numbers. It is a quantifiable, recordable piece of information that feels 'absolute' and real. There is also clear scriptural precedence for using numbers as a measurement. The effect of Peter's sermon in the Acts of the Apostles, for example, is numerically validated by the claim that 3,000 persons were added to the movement following it (Acts 2.41). I can't say that such numbers don't matter to me, because they do, but they don't matter that much.

Thinking both theologically and strategically, however, prompts the realization that church membership isn't an end in itself; it is a way of achieving something else. Similarly, the number of people attending church services isn't a measure of the end itself, but of how many people engaged in a process which had its own purpose. Church leadership teams therefore need to ask the strategic questions, 'What is the purpose?', 'What is the purpose of people coming to church?', 'What is the purpose of people becoming members?' The act of asking these questions is in itself important, the effort required to identify what it is we are hoping to achieve week by week and year by year is an effort that matters, regardless of the answers. However, for now let me suggest some answers. People attend church to worship God, to put God at the centre of everything, to come humbly before their maker and be lost in wonder, love and praise. People become members of the Church because this is a way of following Christ, the Son of the living God. It is in the community of others that people learn to become who they are meant to be, to learn to love God, each other and themselves as they were created to love, to be open to the healing, restoring and completing work of the Holy Spirit as they are 'changed from glory into glory'. Membership figures and attendance figures cannot communicate this on their own. It is essential, however, to know that this is why these figures matter, otherwise the reason why people are made members or the way that the Church seeks to attract worshippers will be fundamentally compromised. My own belief is that if we keep our eye on the purpose the numbers will take care of themselves; the challenge is to ask, 'Given that purpose, what does success look like?', 'What are the signs of a congregation that is worshipping God?', 'Where is the evidence in the Church that membership is leading to discipleship?' These are fascinating theological questions that subvert the whole language of strategy while taking on board its challenge to be honest and clear about what it is we labour for.

The answers to these questions must be clarified even in their 'subverted' form in order to make strategic judgements: 'How should church resources be used?', and in order to monitor and evaluate (control) ministerial efforts: 'What does success look like?' Of course there is no guarantee that clear goals will ensure success, or that failing to achieve particular goals is a sign of pathetic failure. Many of the outcomes of the efforts of the church leadership team lie outside their control. All that can be done is to be faithful; in particular, ministers need the salutary reminder that they can pipe all they like but people still won't dance (Matthew 11.17). Nonetheless, unless intentions can be clearly and precisely known, strategic judgements are difficult to make, and control becomes impossible. Unless it is known what it is we want to achieve, we will find being faithful impossible because we will have nothing to be faithful about.

What then constitutes a 'well-formed objective'? The following is from the world of Neuro Linguistic Programming which takes seriously the place of the unconscious in our goal setting. The objective has to be:

- in the positive (a positive statement of intent rather than a negative one);
- within your control to make the difference (can't depend on others who do not share your hopes);
- specific and detailed, perhaps with a real visceral feel to it; what does it feel, smell, taste, sound, look like?;
- compelling – it has got to be something you really want to happen.

I find this most helpful in my personal goal setting; however, the second point is more difficult in working within organizations. It seems to me that one *always* has to set goals that lie in the hands of others. I can't make people come to events I run at the Guy Chester Centre, but I have to make a reasonable judgement that a certain number will, and I need to be precise about that if I am to allocate resources of staff and time, even though no one may come. Noticing that I need to be clear about what I intend but that the outcome isn't wholly mine to achieve is important in managing stress and anxiety. Failure is never simply failure, or success success: it has to be reflected upon and understood. To have a clear, precise, well-formed objective allows me to judge whether I have achieved it. Knowing I have or haven't isn't the end of the matter, but it allows all the helpful questions that are part of a policy cycle in which our previous choices are reviewed and perhaps amended. Sometimes failure is simply what happens; we made all the right choices. We hoped and longed and yet were disappointed. In God's world this is also within his capacity to use and make good of. Death itself, the final human failure, is not an end of God's creative love. 'All things work together for good!' (Romans 8.28).

The miracle question

There is a question that is used in management consultancy, the source of which I don't know. I have tried to email people who seem to claim it as their own, but so far to no avail! So my apologies to those whose idea it was – here it is.

Imagine that you have a problem and that as you sleep one night the problem is solved by a miracle. You awake in the morning unaware that anything has happened. No one tells you. But as you go through the day, you notice that things are different. What are those differences, how can you tell that the miracle has happened?

I have asked this question of myself and others on many occasions, and I'm often moved by the way it releases people's capacity to understand what it is that they really want to happen. I heard one minister talking about the church where they served. They described the day the miracle happened and as they walked in their imagination into the entrance of the church they realized they no longer noticed a Union flag on the notice board. 'Why does that matter?', we enquired. The answer was complex and involved attitudes towards nationality and belonging that lay at the heart of this minister's dis-ease with some aspects of the congregation. 'Why can you no longer see the flag?' one of his colleagues asked. As the conversation continued, we realized that the flag hadn't actually been taken down, it had simply been lost in the mass of other national flags from all around the world. Not only had we discovered something of the difficulties that lay at the heart of ministry, but we had also come up with a way forward for solving them. 'I noticed that the church was full of flowers,' another minister on another occasion said. 'Who had put them there?' we enquired, inviting her to be more specific. 'All the children and their parents.' 'Why is that important to you?' 'Well, in the church only three people are ever allowed to do the flowers.' Another noticed the smell of coffee, apparently superficial, but as we reflected upon it, all sorts of interesting answers emerged. Issues of quality, hospitality, cultural relevance – and a liking for decent coffee!

Forming a clear picture of what success will look like, one that employs not only thoughts but also feelings and senses, has the potential to release creative solutions to intractable problems and can provide compelling reasons to face up to the presenting challenges.

Control

How do you measure the immeasurable? The key to the policy cycle is the process of monitoring and evaluation that goes on. After struggling to define the objectives that the goals require, strategies are identified which it is believed will help in achieving those objectives, which in turn enables tasks and actions to be determined to fulfil that strategy. Then the question is posed: 'Is the strategy working?' Knowing the answer to this enables a return to all the preceding questions that were asked and all the choices that were made, in order to refine them. Were the goals and objectives realistic? Were the strategies and tasks effective? What other goals might be identified to achieve the mission? What other strategies might be needed to achieve the specific goals? Failure in this may be seen as only feedback; it is to be welcomed and understood, and not regretted.

The policy cycle is a continual process of questioning and choosing in which the mission is kept uppermost, and, without giving up, assesses the effectiveness and helpfulness of the decisions made in the light of the chosen means of control. But this is the challenge; control of something as complex as the miracle of the Church is not a straightforward matter of counting numbers. To be able to describe what success should look like can provide some hints. The kind of goals and objectives that are set in a church, however, means that most ministerial outcomes are not measurable in an empirical or otherwise straightforward way. Because it is difficult, some simply ignore them and measure something else instead. They will speak of all the things they have done, and not what they have achieved by the doing. They will count heads, or income, or something easy to add up. But this is missing the point. Discernment of God's presence of the fruits of the Spirit is an essential skill of Christian leadership. 'Thus you will know them by their fruits,' Jesus tells us (Matthew 7.20). The fruits of the Spirit are peace, patience, kindness, self control, Paul reminds us (Galatians 5.22–23). When we have the courage to ask, 'What will success look like?' in ministry, we create a theologically challenging and stimulating problem which demands a spiritually mature process of discernment.

Because of the degree of complexity involved in good management, sometimes ministers and priests question whether they should be in the business of management at all. They are right, I believe, to worry about such a question. The professionalization of the ministry is a complex and controversial process. Clergy may have much to learn from a more articulate and conscious approach to skills, competencies, attitudes and knowledge that comprise the modern professional. They also, however, have much to lose. The vocation is as much about 'being' as 'doing', about being in love with God and reflecting in their lives the immeasurable richness of God's grace and affection for them. However, in this one area if no other, the priest or minister brings to the policy cycle the heart of their calling of spiritual discernment. With the leadership of their congregation they ask, 'Where do we see God in all this?', 'Where do we discern the fruits of his Spirit?' The answers will not be in numbers, though numbers will matter; they will be in the hard-to-define but immensely important stories of God's grace working in the lives of people who have come closer to him.

Reward

Rewarding those who seek for no reward, but 'knowing that they do God's will' isn't easy – but it is an essential aspect of our strategic thinking. It helps us 'think through the shot', as the golfers say. We see through from vision to outcome and thus we have a better sense of the whole. Planning what you will do if you succeed is a helpful way of motivating yourself and sharpening up your understanding of what you hope to achieve in a way that you will notice:

- It helps us recognize all the people who have been brave, worked hard, overcome resistances and who need valuing.
- It allows us to focus our success on God in celebration and thanksgiving.
- It gives us permission to return to new challenges and problems with the confidence that we can actually make a difference.

Rewards need to make sense of vision quite as much as every other step on the hierarchy of ideas. When reward is about our Christian ministry, it doesn't mean we should be ignored and taken for granted; rather, our gratitude and pleasure in success has to be celebrated as part of our overall gratitude at the goodness of God, who not only calls but equips, who not only equips but guides and inspires.

Conclusion

Experience has taught me that some ministers are immediately drawn to the approach to management in ministry that I have outlined here. They find the idea that problems can be solved, that we can think positively and logically about complex issues, compelling and useful. I am also aware that some ministers are instantly 'turned off'. I know that many ministers lead without any of these tools in ways that leave me breathless with admiration. I have no brief that says, 'Use such approaches or count yourself inadequate!' However, I do have this strong belief that skills and knowledge gained in places other than the Church will almost certainly have a place in the Church, but they need ministers to think about them carefully, be theologically alert, spiritually aware, and conscious that their overriding purpose in life is to do everything to God's glory in response to his extraordinary love.

Notes

1 George A. Lindbeck, *The Nature of Doctrine: Religion and Theology in a Postliberal Age*, London: SPCK, 1984.

2 G. Johnson, K. Scholes and R. Whittington, *Exploring Corporate Strategy*, Harlow: FT/Prentice Hall, 2006.

3 Johnson, *Exploring*, p. 13. In the example which follows I have taken the liberty of swapping around their terms for mission and vision.

4 Johnson, *Exploring* comes in various versions and the following is not based on one version in particular but upon my own composite after ten years' use and reflection. I have recently bought the 2006 edition which has a number of useful additions, and formal quotes are from that.

5 A process of reflective practice developed by Fr Joseph Leon Cardijn which can be summarized as Experience–Analysis–Reflection–Response.

6 Johnson, *Exploring*, p. 13.

7 J. Moltmann, *Theology of Hope*, London: SCM Press, 1983.

8 M. S. Peck, *The Road Less Travelled: The New Psychology of Love, Traditional Values and Spiritual Growth*, London: Rider, 1997.

7

Ministerial Accountability and Continuing Vocational Development

ROGER WIIG

Introduction

Many professions within the secular world are recognizing the increasingly complex nature of the issues they face as they offer their services to societies experiencing rapid social, economic and cultural change. They are defining what is expected of a person working within their profession and they are recognizing the benefits that accrue from establishing agreed standards of performance. They expect members of their profession to be committed to using their skills and knowledge with wisdom and care, to keeping abreast of changes and innovative ideas for effective performance, and to developing capacities for working alongside others. They also expect members to reflect on their actual performances in each respect and hold to the values, goals and requirements of their professional community. Continuing Professional Development (CPD), often a requirement for the practitioner's recognition by their professional association, is seen as a way of maintaining not only the quality and usefulness of the services offered by the profession but also the confidence and trust the public has in its members.

Christian Churches in the West, where confidence in the Church is in serious decline, are beginning to recognize a similar need to clarify the expectations they have of their ministry agents and to encourage them to reflect on what it is that they actually do in exercising ministry. Clergy are increasingly conscious of changes in the roles they have in the community and are beginning to look tentatively for support from their colleagues, but there is a long way to go before lifelong learning and regulated, supervised accountability become the norm for all clergy. In Methodist churches of the 'secular West' there are only a few examples of a formal requirement for CPD including supervision.

Accountability, ethics and ministry

Thoroughgoing reflection on practice and the development of an ethical approach to ministry has been in place in the Uniting Church in Australia (UCA) for the past ten years. The Uniting Church (a denomination combining former Methodist, Presbyterian and Congregational Churches) produced two major documents (based on earlier work done by the Presbyterian Church of Aotearoa, New Zealand): the *Code of Ethics and Ministry Practice*, 2000 and *Pastoral Supervision: Introducing a Process of Reflection on Ministry Experience*, 2001. Beginning from the UCA's *Basis of Union* the documents identify the nature of the Christian community, the particular place that ministers have within it, the nature and seriousness of the pastoral relationships, and the requirement that 'the minister will embody integrity, trust and compassion'. They define the pastoral relationship, recognizing that that relationship is 'concerned for maturity in Christian life and for the fullness of life for all people' and that in that relationship, the minister 'seeks to express an ethic of care which includes nurturing the other person's power over their own life as they relate to others and to God'. In all of this they affirm that the guide to behaviour is to be found 'through the vows of commissioning and ordination'. The *Code* identifies eight principal areas of ministry:

1 Relationships *with colleagues* that respect the rights and responsibilities of those who share in leadership (both lay and ordained) and acknowledge the call and placement of other ministers (both men and women) 'as equals in standing and responsibility'.
2 Teaching that represents accurately the 'teachings of the scriptures and the church'. 'Ministers have an obligation to present the gospel of Jesus Christ, guided by the witness to Christ in the scripture, to take seriously the tradition of faith and worship of the catholic church; and to share that faith in the language and forms of the particular worshipping community and to address its issues'. That requires among other things that ministers 'be open to challenge and correction from colleagues'.
3 Relationships *with church councils* that require ministers to respect the guidance and decisions of the councils of the Church and maintain accountability within the discipline of the Church.
4 Competence *in ministry* that requires ministers to undertake appropriate continuing education and recognize the limits to their own professional competence. The *Code* states that where ministers are forced by circumstances to provide care beyond their normal competence they shall: 'discuss this with their supervisor; seek guidance from a person

with appropriate competence and where warranted see opportunities to develop the appropriate skills'.

5 Professionalism that places 'boundary pegs' around the pastoral relationship and identifies the expectation that relationships are to be conducted in a professional manner.

6 Confidentiality that recognizes the need for particular behaviours in particular settings but does not allow the minister to avoid responsibilities. The *Code* gives very practical guidance on how ministers are to treat information they receive in a pastoral relationship and within the processes of the Church.

7 Self-care that requires ministers to maintain their physical, spiritual and emotional health; to participate in supervision; to give adequate priority to their relationship with their family; and to nurture personal relationships which assist them to achieve wholeness.

8 Supervision that is regular and professional and encourages ministers 'to maintain their professionalism in difficult circumstances'. Such supervision, the *Code* says, 'is intended to assist ministers maintain the boundaries of the pastoral relationships and quality of ministry'.

Besides publishing the document and making it available to all people who are exercising a recognized, formal ministry, the Uniting Church in Australia requires all ministers to attend rigorous training courses on the *Code* and to be clear about its implications for their ministry. While there are some differences in the way the *Code* is implemented by the State Synods, 'supervision' is seen as a normal part of ministerial practice. Ministers are required to report to their Presbytery that they are under supervision, and their Supervisor, while maintaining complete confidentiality on the content of supervision sessions, is expected to report that the supervisee is working appropriately within the supervision sessions. The system has been enriched by the practices of the theological seminaries where the expectation that supervision is a normal part of ministry is upheld as the students develop theological and pastoral skills. Students assigned to parishes for pastoral education are supervised by the minister of the parish, who in turn meets with other ministers performing this particular function for the seminary, and is required to present case studies on the way in which they are supervising the student and on the issues that are arising for the minister in their work with the student. The skills developed in this exercise are then available to the wider Church as those with training take opportunities to pass on to others what they have learned about reflecting on the practice of ministry. All of this builds an environment where supervision is seen as normal and as contributing to the development of the skills of ministry, the mental and spiritual well-being of the ministers, and the support that ministers offer to members of the congregations they serve during their time of ministry.

The Methodist Church in New Zealand, Te Haahi Weteriana, with similar concerns, has a brief document entitled 'Ethical Standards for Ministry' which sets out the 'Church's position on standards of conduct for people, clergy and lay, who undertake ministry in the name of the church'. It is 'a document of commitment rather than of intent' leaving little room for clergy reluctance. It identifies the responsibilities that those who minister in the name of the Church have to:

1 those to whom they offer pastoral care;
2 the Church;
3 colleagues;
4 the wider community; and
5 themselves.

The Methodist Churches in Great Britain, South Africa and the United States have yet to be as firm and clear, although the Church in the United States is proposing recommendations to its Conference that would make peer supervision a requirement for all deacons and elders. The British Methodist Conference is trialling an 'Annual Development Review' that seeks specifically 'to respond to a Minister's need for professional and vocational development and training'. A tentative, minimalist scheme, it is being offered in the hope that it might encourage clergy to see the value of reflective praxis and so overcome what appears to be fairly significant resistance to the idea of collegial accountability. In South Africa, the Methodist Church has recently (September 2007) launched a Human Resource Unit which, among other matters, will be looking at the accountability, care and supervision of the work of ministers.

Part of the issue for all three Churches is how the role of the ordained clergy is defined in their regulations. In South Africa, ministers are not defined as employees but rather are in a covenant relationship with the Church. The same is true for the Church in Great Britain. The latter recently accepted a report entitled 'What is a Presbyter?' that seeks to clarify the 'characteristics', the 'tasks' and the 'accountabilities' of a presbyter, by pulling together various strands of tradition in the Church's foundational documents. A presbyter is, the paper argues: 'a person of faith, committed to living as a disciple of Jesus Christ who has a strong sense of God's calling to ministry, which is tested and affirmed by the Church'. He or she is 'of good character, committed to the pursuit of holiness and life-long learning, and faithful to apostolic doctrine'; 'obedient, accepting Connexional discipline, "our doctrines" and the principle of stationing'. He or she is 'firmly rooted within Methodist tradition, but draws on and is enriched by other ecclesiastical traditions'. In other words: 'A presbyter is a "whole" person, interconnected with others through family, friendship or other close relationships.'

The paper lists the various tasks of a presbyter and then says a presbyter is accountable first to God, then to the Church – 'through a "covenant relationship" with the Conference in which a presbyter accepts the authority and support of the Conference and is in turn entrusted with representing them to others', and to ordained colleagues 'through "watching over each other in love" communally and collegially in *ad hoc* relationships and groups, staff meetings, Ministerial Sessions of Synod, and the Ministerial Session of Conference'. Finally a presbyter is accountable to others – 'through behaving with integrity, competence and according to the best standards of practice towards those to whom she or he ministers'.

All this spells out an ideal but does little to meet resistance and scepticism about how the Church might facilitate collegial accountability and continuing vocational development. All is not well among the clergy. 'An unacceptably high proportion of Methodist Circuit ministers feel emotionally exhausted and stressed by their ministry.'[1] Church courts struggle with what to do about clergy who are ineffective or who step over pastoral boundaries. Ministers struggle with the ever-increasing demands that purportedly 'leave little time for ministry' or for finding 'balance' in a healthy lifestyle. Sadly, too many are caught up into conflict from the power games that are inevitably played in some congregations or from personal failure to maintain pastoral boundaries. Little time is spent in theological reflection on pastoral practice. Skills in group work are limited and only a minority commit themselves to working with others so that life and work are shaped more and more in the pattern of Jesus' way.

Professional priorities

There is a general recognition that 'continuing professional development' and 'lifelong learning' are personal responsibilities of ministers, but they are given little priority. There is little evidence that the collegiality that John Wesley recognized as being important for his preachers is a central practical commitment of those who minister within circuits or alongside neighbouring circuits or parishes that are close enough to one another to work together. Even though ministry is becoming more difficult in the secular societies of the West, ministers find it difficult to talk with one another about how they actually minister, let alone how they might improve ministerial performance in this changing context by recognizing the potential that the Methodist system offers for collegial professional development. What should be opportunity for support and deep conversation ends in silence. The danger at this point is that clergy lose a sense of identity and are at risk of 'burnout'.[2] Richard Busch, in an article in *The Christian Century*, says:

> I suspect, however, that behind this silence is finally this: the gospel is not the centre of our lives, and our spiritual life is disconnected from the things that interest, worry and excite us. We have so many pressing interests, priorities and passions in our lives that we no longer seek first the kingdom. We lack the singleness of heart to be attentive to God. In our desire to be like the people around us, we emphasise the outward doing dimensions over the inward being dimensions of Christian living . . . Faith is not a thing one 'loses', we merely cease to shape our lives by it. And that is the real question for clergy: how is our faith to shape the way we live?[3]

Yet, in spite of the tired questioning about what models could be effective and how they could be made workable in settings where there is little trust and a great reluctance to be open about real difficulties, clergy have neither abandoned the discussion of the need for ministerial accountability and continuing vocational development nor given up the search for effective models of collegial interaction that would enable peers to talk with openness and trust about the issues they are really facing.

Gwen Purushotham, in a paper entitled 'Supervision as a Means of Grace' presented to the Oxford Institute of Theology in 2007, spoke of responses to a draft recommendation from the United Methodist Church's General Board of Higher Education and Ministry to recommend peer supervision for all deacons and itinerant elders. She commented: 'the Commission's recommendation and the responses to it depict a community that is struggling with the need and desire to be accountable while at the same time expressing resistance and scepticism about engaging itself in such a process'. Her conviction is that 'theological reflection on the church's practice of supervision is urgently needed to address the issues of trust, authority and status of supervision in the church's life and ministry'. Her beliefs are that 'the suspicion and confusion that surround supervision in the church is due in large part to a lack of theological grounding of our practice' and that a 'clear articulation of our theology of supervision' is needed, and that that clarity is found in 'Wesley's understanding of sanctification'.[4]

Much is to be admired in her attempt to 'provoke a conversation about an area of theology and practice that must be engaged thoughtfully and systematically' if the Church is to rethink the practice of supervision. Her suggestions about the way a theology of sanctification aids our understanding of the 'gradual process of growth in love brought about through God's transforming and saving work in us and our response to God's gracious action in our lives' are valuable. She says:

> If sanctification is a gradual and life-long process in which we are being continually transformed into the likeness of Christ, then supervision rooted in this theological assumption would be characterised by attentiveness to identity formation, patience with the process of growth and intentional relationships, structures and disciplines that support this process.

Theological and contractual standards for ministerial practice

In everyday practice, is it theology or is it the covenant entered into at the time of ordination that leads to real recognition of the responsibilities that ministers have towards supervision and continuing vocational development? Gwen Purushotham would seem to say the one; the Uniting Church in Australia's *Code of Ethics and Ministry Practice*[5] would seem to suggest the other. When faced with these ideas of motivation as alternatives, most ministers would turn away from choosing one against the other. On the one hand, they would wish to say that finding a safe place in which they can honestly explore their conduct in pastoral relationships with others is more of an issue than is the ability to articulate a particular theological justification or name a particular doctrine justifying their actions. This could lead them to favour supervision as it is often practised in secular professions.

On the other hand, they would recognize – when faced with the challenge of making a choice in just this way – that as people who see themselves as followers of the way of Jesus they should be willing to ask questions about the extent to which their activities as ministry agents have integrity with 'the way'. And that would recognize that ministers, of all people, should be able to ask those questions, as Jesus and his disciples did when gathered as a group and when gathered together with others whose companionship and counsel they sought.

What is missing is a clear understanding that there are, as in other professions, standards in ministry that might reasonably be expected of clergy in the performance of their ministry. While none has a mandate from any Church to set standards for their colleagues, the concept is worthy of exploration. The document 'What is a Presbyter?' adopted by the Conference of the Methodist Church in Great Britain,[6] as indicated above, seeks to clarify the 'characteristics', the 'tasks' and the 'accountabilities' of a presbyter, but it sets out no measurable standards of performance against which ministers might make an assessment of their ministry that would lead to identifying appropriate goals for continuing education, and no way of identifying what a circuit (or parish) might reasonably expect of a minister. The identifying of professional 'standards' might also sharpen the work of seminaries and those charged with training ministers. Such standards would describe the knowledge, understanding, abilities and values or motivations necessary for effective, ethical ministry. They could not prescribe *how* this should be done; they would simply provide a framework and common language that would enable ministers to identify, assess and strengthen their professional commitment to ministry.

At the heart of the 'standards' should be a commitment to reflective practice and growth that honours God's love and his example on earth in the life of Christ. Beyond this there should be:

o a measurable commitment to personal development and participation in society;
o a clear ability to work alongside lay people already engaged in mission in the local church;
o a capacity and willingness to encourage the worship and mission of local congregations;
o a willingness to accept the obligation of regular consultation with the staff team into which they are appointed; and
o a capacity to foster positive and productive relationships within the community.

All of this must have its focus on what the minister actually does in working supportively with the congregation as they express their capacity to worship and to grow in their discipleship, living out the values of God's kingdom in the way of Christ. For this work to be effective, the disciplines within the minister's life must give attention to prayer, study, pastoral care and the management of time. Each of these key aspects of the minister's work is an appropriate area for reflection in the supervision process.

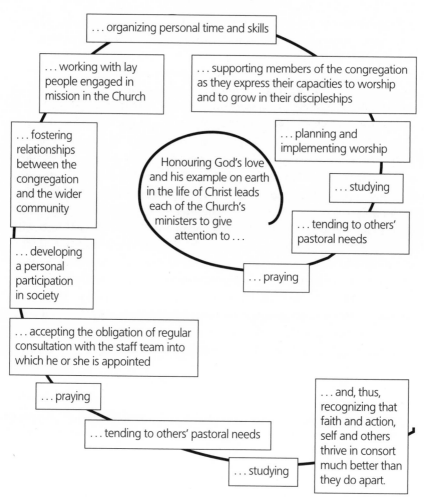

In that process the minister must not only be able to state clearly what specific action he or she takes, but also the expectations that he or she has in this aspect of ministry. Expressing these ideas in diagram form (see above) as well as in words brings to mind not only the day-to-day tasks of ministry but also the memories:

o that each task interweaves with others;
o that faith and action thrive in consort much better than they do apart;
o that self without others will not fulfil the mission dreamed of by the Church;

o that ministry is about tasks that may seem to repeat what has been done before – but each time they are carried out in faith their meaning is refreshed.

Reflection on these aspects of ministry may identify those things that a minister needs to know and understand – and those things that the British Methodist Church is now grouping under the concept Exploring Discipleship, Extending Vocation (EDEV).

Theology and practice cannot be separated, but how do we inspire, encourage and enable clergy to engage in an appropriate method that provides a safe environment for in-depth reflection on the practice of ministry? The word 'supervision' for some implies a hierarchy and a demanding authority; it may be felt to be an imposition and a way of 'getting at' non-performing clergy. Peer group supervision and co-consultancy groups take away some of the feeling that the work is something imposed by others and clearly puts the initiative and power into the hands of those who choose to participate. Here, the Uniting Church in Australia's paper on pastoral supervision is helpful. It recognizes that the word 'supervision' may be used to describe three different working relationships:

1 *Formative supervision* involves a learning relationship where the wisdom and experience of two or more people meet in constructive interaction; normally one person will have more experience of ministry than the other.
2 *Organizational supervision* is defined in the Constitution of the UCA (par. 15) as: 'Ministers and Lay Pastors will be responsible to a Presbytery and Synod in matters of faith and discipline, and the Presbytery or other appointing body for the exercise of their ministry.'
3 *Consultative supervision* is a supportive and collegial relationship which may be expressed one to one, or in a small group context of mutual accountability.

The document says:

Supervision is a safe, confidential relationship which provides a regular opportunity to reflect on our work and professional relationships. It only works where an atmosphere of trust is built up. Supervisee and supervisor are each responsible for building that trust by approaching the other with openness.

The desired outcome of truly pastoral supervision is a continuing enhancement of the ministry offered. Along with this can go increased self-respect, released potential, the capacity to see, feel and hear what has not been seen, felt or heard, and the bonuses of increased health and well-being and increased effectiveness in ministry. Research shows a high correlation between good supervision and vocational satisfaction. Good supervision supports, challenges, encourages learning, self-knowledge, professional development, good use of resources and time, and respect for boundaries. Every supervision relationship is unique and needs its own covenant. The focus of supervision is on actual events, on real, living, ministry situations and experiences.[7]

Peer coaching

Interestingly, the idea of coaching is becoming increasingly popular in the secular world and is now often recommended in situations where supervision would have been recommended in the past. The secular world recognizes the value of scrutinizing and updating language that has become jargonized and concepts that have become less favoured than they once were. It implies a method of interaction that tutors rather than controls, that trains rather than manages, that encourages interaction and progression rather than gives oversight and direction. The idea of coaching seems to offer a more appropriate way of describing the activities of involvement and growth that could be achieved among peers joined by their commitment to the faith proclaimed in the Gospels and their contractual relationships with the Church. For ministers, the idea of coaching enables both the theological and the covenantal motivations for continuing vocational development to be named simultaneously. For ministers, ideas of peer coaching enable a striving for the equality and fairness offered those who would follow the way of Jesus that are intrinsic to Gospel stories; and they enable a sensing of the healthiness and strength of the promise that 'those who lose their life for my sake, and for the sake of the gospel, will save it' (Mark 8.35).

Effective peer coaching may take place informally and involve a limited number of people. It may also be seen as a method which may be formalized for a larger group. My own formal peer coaching experience has involved a peer group of colleagues who met with the goal of gaining greater clarity on what each person was doing both as an individual and as a member of the group who employed him or her, and why he or she was doing things this way. We all needed to bring openness, honesty, trust, listening skills, responding skills and patience to the group. We:

o met at stated intervals over a period of time (but ideally, participants in such a group will accept that members may request additional meetings to cope with unforeseen and pressing issues);

o used a written case study method that presented a disciplined report on a problem with which the presenter was grappling, or on an issue with which he or she sought help at the time (but ideally, participants in such a group will know that written words are not the only vehicles through which everyone best expresses their problems, ideas, tensions or hopes);

o agreed on a standard format for presentation and response (but ideally, participants in such a group will recognize that coaching and humanity, by their natures, may interrupt the process but should not be used as excuses for forgetting the goals of co-operation and encouragement).

With this experience in mind, I offer thoughts on providing a safe environment for in-depth reflection with others on the practice of Christian ministry by:

o setting up a peer coaching group;

o using case study methods to describe the concerns that participants wish to bring to the group;

o guiding case study presentations through the meetings of the group.

The purpose of a peer coaching group is to enable group members to encourage each other's continuing assessment of their vocational development by working individually and together on problems, issues and ideas that present themselves through the daily tasks encountered in ministry. If such a group is to be successful, thought should be given to both the purpose and the process at the time of its establishment and to the agreement of all members to a binding covenant of confidentiality.

At the time of the establishment of the group, and intermittently through its life, it is extremely beneficial – and perhaps essential – to organize workshops to discuss the practice of the group. A common method is that of having a meeting in which the process, rather than an individual member's heartfelt concerns, will be the principal topic. For such a workshop, a member of the group prepares a case study along the lines that will be followed in a usual meeting but on a topic that is not, for that member, of present concern. At the beginning of the workshop a 'moderator' is appointed to perform the usual tasks of guiding the group. Then the group identifies one of its members as a 'process observer'. This person's primary task is that of recording the process followed, noting how the group works together and whether or not it is clear about the goals of the discussion, recording those who take initiatives and what those initiatives achieve for the group, identifying any controls that have been applied to the discussion, and noting any significant transitions. In other words, what helped and what hindered? When the presentation and discussion are concluded, the moderator invites the process observer to report back. Then, group members share their reactions, identifying ways in which their understanding of helpful and unhelpful communication dynamics has been strengthened or changed. Finally, they exchange promises to temper future group discussions with the knowledge gained.

Case studies for peer coaching groups should be recorded in brief form by the presenter (by using one or several of the writing, list-making, drawing, diagram-making, or PowerPoint styles, that enables the presenter to feel that she or he has described the problem or issue or idea clearly and succinctly) using the following points as the framework:

- Describe the nature of the problem or issue or idea being presented (as it seems to you).
- List the people who are affected by the problem or issue or idea.
- List your reasons for wishing to deal with this concern.
- Tell the story, briefly, of the way in which your feelings and actions are controlled or curtailed by a lack of resolution of the problem or issue or idea.
- Give a considered opinion of the way in which other people's feelings, actions and roles might be being controlled or curtailed by a lack of resolution of the problem or issue or idea.
- Offer an estimation of the degree of urgency there is in dealing with the problem or issue or idea.
- Give reasons for the degree of urgency you suggest.
- Set out your dream remedy.
- Set out the dream remedies of others involved in the situation or affected by the issue or idea.
- List the consequences for yourself and the church community if the problem is resolved, or the issue or idea is understood, in the way you desire.
- List the consequences for yourself and the church community if the problem is not resolved, or the issue or idea is not understood, in the way you desire.
- Name the nature of the help being sought from the peer group by completing the sentence 'I would be helped in dealing with this by . . .'
- Write your name, the date on which you will be presenting the case study, and the names of those to whom you are expecting to present the concern, at the foot of the page.

- Make sufficient copies of your case study for each of the members of the peer coaching group to which you will be presenting your material, if you have written it on paper. Make sure your equipment is functioning well, if, for example, you have prepared a PowerPoint presentation of your material.

The following format for presentation and response in a peer coaching group could be taken as standard, in the first instance at least.

1 The group meets, determines the length of the meeting and appoints a moderator for the day.
2 The moderator (i) begins the session with prayer, (ii) seeks renewal of the group's commitment to the covenant of confidentiality that would have formed a part of the group's establishment, (iii) guides the group through the process, and (iv) keeps an eye on the time.
3 The presenter reads the prepared case study to the other participants.
4 The presenter shares any further details of the story behind the case study and sets out her or his goals for the discussion.
5 Up to 15 minutes are taken on questions seeking clarification from the presenter on the nature of the problem or issue or idea being presented and on the presenter's goals for the session.
6 Approximately 30 to 45 minutes are taken to respond to the problem or issue or idea of the presenter by addressing questions such as 'How might this issue be addressed?', 'What options for action does the presenter have?' (Participants may be drawn to offer experiences of their own that have involved similar problems, issues or ideas. If they do, they should remember to keep their personal comment brief and relevant, for they are here to encourage the presenter's progress rather than to comfort or praise themselves.)
7 The presenter is invited to identify those options that have been helpful and mull over what actions she or he will take as a result of the discussion.
8 The group takes ten minutes to share ways in which the discussion has helped them understand actions which they themselves have taken in the past or ideas on which they may act in the future.
9 Group members offer the presenter any specific forms of help or support they are willing to give.
10 If the presenter desires it, a date is set for a review of the outcome of the problem or issue or idea that has been presented and the identification of any follow-up still required.
11 The presenter gathers in any distributed copies or materials of her or his case study.

12 The moderator closes the session with prayer.

Such a process offers a safe environment for in-depth reflection with others on the practice of Christian ministry, encouraging a greater focus on ministerial accountability and continuing vocational development. The Church has a responsibility and right to proscribe the contractual relationship with ministers and to expect ministerial performance at appropriate standards, but each minister has the responsibility of working towards the greater integration of the theology they espouse and the ministry they offer.

Notes

1 John M. Haley and Lesley J. Francis, *British Methodism: What Circuit Ministers Really Think*, Peterborough: Epworth Press, 2006, p. 227.

2 Douglas Brandon, *Vocational Dissonance – A Grounded Theory of Vocational Distress Among Ministers of the Uniting Church in Australia*, PhD thesis, Griffith University, Brisbane, January 1996.

3 Richard A. Busch, 'A Strange Silence', in *The Christian Century*, 112:10, 1995, pp. 316ff.

4 Gwen Purushotham, 'Supervision as a Means of Grace', unpublished paper presented to the Oxford Institute of Theology, August 2007.

5 *Code of Ethics and Ministry Practice* (for Ministers of the Word, Deacons, Youth Workers, Community Ministers and Lay Pastors in the Uniting Church in Australia [whether in approved placements or not]), Uniting Church in Australia, approved by the 9th Assembly, July 2000.

6 British Methodist Church, Methodist Conference, 2002 Report, 'What is a Presbyter?', Peterborough, 2002.

7 *Pastoral Supervision: Introducing a Process of Reflection on Ministry Experience*, Uniting Church in Australia, September 2001, p. 3.

Living with the Consequences – Being and Doing

SHERYL ANDERSON

Introduction

During 2005, as part of a bigger study, I conducted a survey among church members in the (now superseded) London South East District of the Methodist Church, to ask them what they thought made a minister (presbyter), and more specifically, what made a 'good' minister. Not good in the sense of morally good or well behaved, but good in the sense of possessing certain qualities or virtues.

The survey was less concerned with what a presbyter is and does, than with how congregations perceive presbyters. It was specifically designed to explore congregants' understanding of ministry. In the debate within Methodism about presbyters, and all the literature and the many studies about ministry and ministers, there do not seem to be any documents that seek to consult church members about the nature or quality of the ministry that they receive. There are many congregational studies, especially in the United States[1] and many theories that explain congregational behaviour and idiosyncrasies. One highly influential work is Hopewell's *Congregation: Stories and Structures*,[2] which advocates a symbolic or cultural approach, stemming from the author's belief that every congregation has its own meaning, expressed in a story. Ammerman,[3] however, outlines a number of approaches to studying congregations, designed to help church leaders and others make sense of the forces at work in individual Christian communities. In these instances, whether studies adopt sociological, ethnographic or anthropological approaches, the congregation is the subject of the exercise and the information is for those looking in from the outside.

Similarly, there are many theological and educational works about the ministry, about what it means, how to do it, why do it, and who should do it. There are books to help ministers be more effective and efficient, and many works to help congregational revival and the development of mission and service. There is also much theological reflection on the nature of ministry. Within British Methodism, one recent publication by Haley and Francis[4] explores the attitudes and beliefs of circuit ministers about their work and the structure of the Methodist Church nationally. However, in all this plethora of material there is nothing that actually asks congregations what they think ministers are about and what they value most about the ministry they have experienced. The intention of this chapter is to go a little way towards redressing the balance.

Until relatively recently, everyone in the Methodist Church assumed that they knew what a Methodist minister was. Then, in 1993, the Methodist Conference agreed to reopen the Methodist Diaconate Order (previously the Wesley Deaconesses) as an order of ministry, and suddenly Methodism found itself with a need to clarify the situation. People once referred to simply as ministers were now presbyters (to distinguish them from deacons), but most Methodist congregations did not have much to do with deacons, and so continued to refer to the presbyter as 'the minister'. The Church, having established what a deacon is and does, then realized that, although they all assumed that they knew what a presbyter is and does, actually they might not. Thus began some interesting and considered thinking.

For the purposes of this chapter, when I use the term 'minister', I am referring to presbyters with pastoral charge: which, arguably, continues to be the way the term is understood by the vast majority of Methodists.

The context of the study

Ministry in the Methodist Church

The 1932 Deed of Union makes the following statement about ministry in the Methodist Church:

> Christ's ministers in the church are stewards in the household of God and shepherds of his flock. Some are called and ordained to this sole occupation and have a principal and directing part in these great duties but they hold no priesthood differing in kind from that which is common to all the Lord's people and they have no exclusive title to the preaching of the Gospel or the care of souls. These ministries are shared by them with others to whom also the Spirit divides his gifts severally as he wills.

It is the universal conviction of the Methodist people that the office of the Christian ministry depends upon the call of God who bestows the gifts of the Spirit, the grace and fruit which indicate those whom he has chosen.[5]

In an effort to stress the notion of 'the priesthood of all believers', this text uses the terms 'ministers' and 'ministries' in a confused way: a confusion which typifies the ambivalence with which Methodists continue to emphasize the notion of the ministry of the whole people of God (sometimes called 'every member ministry' in other contexts) and yet still refer to 'the' minister or 'our' minister, as meaning the ordained presbyter in that locality. To make matters worse, Methodist ministers are deployed connexionally; that is, they are neither called by a local congregation nor licensed to a local parish, but stationed by the Methodist Conference. Ministers are sent by the Church to represent the Church (among other things) to a local circuit. This additional layer of significance compounds the confusion. Methodism continues to struggle to understand how the principle of 'no priesthood differing in kind' can be held together with a connexional understanding of ministry for and on behalf of the whole Church. The report to the 1988 Methodist Conference, 'The Ministry of the People of God'[6] attempted to address this issue and to establish a balance between lay and ordained ministries in the Church. Despite this, however, the inherited contradictions hinted at in the Deed of Union continue to influence the way in which different ministerial roles are understood and exercised in Methodism today. The most recent report to the 2002 Methodist Conference, entitled, 'What is a Presbyter?',[7] attempted to clarify further the Methodist Church's current understanding of presbyteral ministry, but reports to Conference do not necessarily reflect actual practice on the ground. Many Methodists understand ministry to be something that primarily concerns the 'minister', and local congregations continue to speak of 'our own minister' when referring to the presbyter in pastoral charge. Furthermore, many presbyters themselves speak in terms 'my ministry', an expression that is rarely used by lay people.

All of this is by way of setting the context for the study, which sought to explore a number of linked issues about Methodist presbyters and the particular ministry to which they are called; and which sought to do so from a distinct viewpoint – that of the people who are largely on the receiving end of presbyters' ministrations. All the literature, reports and studies focus almost exclusively on the minister (presbyter or deacon) from the point of view of the Methodist Church as church: that is, they attempt to offer a theological and ecclesial view of what it means to be a minister. However, as Leslie Griffiths[8] points out, ordinary people also have a view of what it is that makes a minister, and it is not acceptable to dismiss these views as merely illusory or 'folksy' simply because it suits us. There is a longing, he suggests, in people who cry out in their need of ministry, which the Church ignores at its peril. According to Griffiths, the people have a clear understanding of what a minister is:

- A minister is the person who stands up to preach, to conduct funerals, to baptize children, to conduct weddings, to offer bread and wine.
- A minister visits us in our homes and models the Christian life for us.
- A minister takes charge of the words and reminds us of dimensions to human living which, under the pressures of everyday life, are too easily forgotten.[9]

Griffiths freely admits that this assertion is merely an impression based on his considerable experience as a Methodist minister over a long period of time. However, his assertions resonate sufficiently to warrant further investigation. This moves us on to the next issue.

If ordinary people do have a view of what makes a minister, then presumably they also have a view of what makes a 'good'[10] minister; that is, they can differentiate between ministers who perform well and those who perform poorly. However, as the ongoing debate within Methodism (and elsewhere) demonstrates, there is more to ordained ministry than the performance of tasks. Griffiths' list includes ontological behaviours – modelling the Christian life, for example – so if he is correct, can we assume that ordinary people are able to identify 'good' ministers in terms of who they are, as well as in terms of what they do? If they can, and my argument is that they can, the question then is, can we enable ordinary people in congregations to articulate what makes a 'good' minister good?

Continuing vocational development

Until very recently, the Methodist Church in Great Britain ran a scheme of evaluation for ministers called 'Accompanied Self-Appraisal'. The system relied on ministers being willing and able to undertake self-evaluation, with a view to improving their professional practice. Ministers were assigned an 'accompanist', an independent person who supported them through the process, and were encouraged to seek feedback from their congregations on their performance in various aspects of their roles. To enable them to carry out the task appropriately, both ministers and accompanists received training, a proportion of which was devoted to the issue of how to elicit constructive feedback from congregations.

Aside from ministers who avoided or refused participation, one of the biggest obstacles to the scheme being effective was the difficulty that individual congregations and ministers had in developing even-handed processes and impartial criteria by which to give and receive feedback. Much that was offered was subjective, uncritical and facile. Generally, congregations lacked the confidence to articulate constructively where a minister's strengths and weaknesses lay, and were rarely equipped with the skills to offer feedback that was useful to a minister. Similarly, many ministers struggled to find constructive ways to gain the information and affirmation that they needed. Ministers and congregations were reluctant to engage honestly with each other because of fear of exposure on both sides. Consequently, the process was characterized by hesitation and uncertainty. However, it was recognized that, unless congregations are able to give quality, constructive feedback to ministers, the possibility of ministers further developing their gifts and graces is somewhat limited.

Typically, ministers wanting to evaluate their preaching and worship-leading skills, for example, might ask, 'What did you think of this morning's service?' Responses might range from, 'Nice hymns', through, 'I appreciated your word', to 'You need to speak up, some people are hard of hearing.' All of which may be true, but they do not give the minister helpful information about what makes some hymns 'nice', why the word was appreciated, or which people (if any) could not hear. Some ministers did attempt to elicit information that was more constructive, but extracting precisely what you want out of the congregation can be very frustrating. There may be difficulty in separating content from process; so general questions about the structure of the sermon can easily become theological arguments about the substance of the sermon. Furthermore, a minister's active attempts to improve his or her presentation of the gospel can be taken as an opportunity for some congregants to exercise their own particular theological hobbyhorse, or to rehearse their resentments, or to assume that the minister is looking for approval. Coping with such misunderstanding is often very discouraging for the minister – precisely the opposite of what seeking feedback intends to achieve. It can also lead to the views of ordinary people not being taken seriously, the kind of dismissive attitude outlined by Griffiths in the previous section.

This brings us back to the question: is it possible for a congregation to identify the gifts and graces that characterize a 'good' minister, or is their view inevitably too distorted by partialities and prejudices to be helpful? Surely church members know 'good' ministry when they encounter it? To suggest otherwise implies that only ministers have the capacity to assess ministers, a view which, partly because of the ambivalence towards ordained ministry outlined previously, does not sit easily within Methodist culture. However, if it *is* true, then what gifts and graces would congregants identify, and can they be helped to articulate them in a way that is more constructive and helpful to ministers?

Thus, despite the difficulties outlined above, it was my assumption that congregations do know what makes a minister, and do recognize a 'good' minister when they encounter one. Furthermore, I believed that actually there exists a tacit consensus about what makes a minister 'good', and that, under the right circumstances, ordinary people can be enabled to identify the characteristics that make a 'good' minister good.

Outline of the study

Accounts of research studies usually devote considerable time to describing in detail the research process. However, it is impossible to go into the methodology in depth within the confines of this chapter. What follows is a necessarily brief version of the approach used.

The purpose of the study was to consider a number of interlinked questions connected with what members of congregations identify as the characteristics of a 'good' minister, and how members of congregations may be enabled to articulate those characteristics in ways that are positive and constructive for both congregations and ministers. Because of the difficulties of critical analysis as described previously, the research had to identify and describe these attributes in ways that clearly separated them from matters such as personal liking, or categories such as age, gender or marital status.[11] This was a major challenge. Nevertheless, the hypothesis was that it should be possible, by enquiry, to ascertain the necessary, distinct characteristics of ministers that congregations identify as 'good'.

Therefore, the general aim of the research was to:

- test whether the hypothesis was correct;
- identify what those characteristics are;
- help congregants become more critically aware of what they categorize as 'good' ministry;
- consider how such critical awareness can enable congregants to participate more constructively in the ongoing development of ministers.

As the specific purpose of the research was to discover what congregations identify as the characteristics of a 'good' minister, the challenge lay in formulating research questions that elicited these characteristics in a useful and constructive format. As previously described, the tendency is for congregants (and others) to use uncritical descriptions of ministers, for example 'I liked her', or 'He never visited', which can be interpreted as telling us as much about the respondent as they do about the minister. The research questions therefore needed to seek feedback (opinions) from congregations, but be structured in such a way as to obtain discrete data: to be concerned with *who* a minister is, rather than *what* he or she does. Consequently, it was essential to focus on specific research questions, to which specific concrete answers could be given:

- Is there a general view among congregants about what constitutes a 'good' minister?
- Can congregants identify the characteristics of a 'good' minister?
- If so, what are they?
- Are they subject to variables (such as age, gender, race, context, etc.) of the congregants?
- Do people who have a strong attachment to their local Methodist church, and who have held office, have a different opinion about what constitutes a 'good' minister from those who are more loosely connected to the organization?
- Are those who have a long-standing association with their local Methodist church more or less realistic about 'good' ministry than those who are relative newcomers?
- Is the definition of 'good' ministry or a 'good' minister so subjective as to be impossible to establish?

At the time, the London South East District included south east London, Kent, parts of Surrey and west Sussex, and Malta. It consisted of approximately 187 churches (some joint churches with ecumenical partners) grouped into 28 circuits, with 11,635 members, served by 76 ministers. There were in the region of 30,000 people on the community roll. A random survey was the preferred means of collecting data to answer the research questions, and the most efficient and effective means of conducting a large, random survey of congregants' opinions was a questionnaire. However, given the relative inflexibility and unrefined character of data collected using this method, some follow-up interviews were also conducted. Kerlinger[12] suggests that the interview enables the researcher to go deeper into the motivations of respondents and their reasons for responding as they do, which fitted precisely a project designed to discover undisclosed opinions.

Thus, two approaches to collecting data were adopted:

1 An initial quantitative survey to discern the general views of individuals in congregations, from as many local Methodist churches in the London South East District as was practicable, the idea being that this survey would enable potential interviewees to be identified.

2 Follow-up interviews of a sample of respondents to determine values, preferences, attitudes and beliefs in more detail.

For reasons of brevity, this chapter will focus almost entirely on the quantitative survey.

Questionnaire design

The design of the questionnaire was a key issue. Because the concept of a 'good' minister can be seen as a vague and subjective notion, it was important not to invite respondents merely to exercise their own personal prejudices about the subject. However, soliciting genuine opinions about the characteristics of good ministry is no easy matter. The questionnaire could list all sorts of admirable qualities, and respondents could agree with every one of them, which would only confirm that a 'good' minister is omni-competent, omni-skilful, and, like Jesus, without sin! This seemed both unrealistic and unhelpful. Consequently, the questionnaire attempted to focus on specific information in a way that carefully operationalized the purposes of the research.

The initial part of the questionnaire was designed to elicit information about the respondent: gender, age, ethnicity, length of attachment to the Church, regularity of worship, degree of participation in church structures and activities. The second part sought information about the respondents' opinions, asking them to reflect specifically on their experience of a 'good' minister (or not) and then to give feedback on the qualities and characteristics that contributed towards their definition of a 'good' minister. The questions in this section focused on discrete characteristics. Another section examined the traditional areas of ministerial activity: pastoral care, teaching, evangelism, leadership, administration, theology and preaching. It invited the respondent to consider what ministers do, and to rank the relative strengths of their identified minister in those areas. The next section moved away from considering an identified individual, to a more general focus, and asked respondents to express opinions about 'good' ministers, which elicited qualities to do with leadership style. Other questions considered characteristics related to personal values and ideology, both of a 'good' minister and of the respondent. The rationale for the items in these questions is a theory of personality, known as

Transactional Analysis, developed by Eric Berne,[13] which gives an account of human interaction founded on an individual's perception of himself or herself in the world. It is not necessary to describe this complex theory here, but it is useful to note that an underlying assumption in the questionnaire was that 'good' ministers demonstrate healthy personality characteristics such as autonomy, flexibility and attachment, as defined by Berne and others.[14] The last section attempted to discover whether congregants have high expectations of a minister's virtuousness, and the questionnaire finished with an open question, enabling respondents to express freely their own opinions about what qualities were necessary for a 'good' minister to be given that description. Finally, people were asked if they would be willing to participate in a further follow-up interview.

Confidentiality

It was apparent that investigating the notion of a 'good' minister in the context of an organization that struggles, at times, to preserve confidentiality and anonymity, was likely to raise anxiety levels among both congregants and ministers. Therefore, because of the sensitive nature of the matters involved, confidentiality was guaranteed to be a key issue. In order to elicit honest responses, participants needed to be assured that all raw data given would be strictly for the declared purposes of the research, only available to the researcher, held securely, and only in a form that prevents specific individuals from being identified (non-traceability). As will be seen later, this proved to be a key consideration.

Process

A draft questionnaire was piloted in three different Methodist circuits outside of the target area. Feedback was requested on both the content of the questionnaire and the process of completing it. This led to some revisions. At this pilot stage it was encouraging to receive the comments of some respondents, for example, 'It made me sit down for quite a while and think about and assess my relationship with God and the Church and what individual ministers had in fact done for me to enable my growth in Christianity.'

By agreement through the District Superintendents' Meeting, a copy of the final questionnaire (see p. 186), the explanatory letter and a covering letter was sent by email to every Circuit Superintendent in the District other than my own: to reduce bias and for reasons of confidentiality, I decided not to conduct the survey in my own circuit. Circuit Superintendents then distributed them to congregations in their circuit. It is interesting to note that, although members of the District Superintendents' Meeting expressed a willingness to co-operate in the distribution of the questionnaires, they were extremely cautious about the whole process. Some Superintendents felt that they might not be able to assist because of particular difficulties they were experiencing in their own circuits at that time, and others were most concerned about issues of confidentiality and the possibility of stirring up trouble and harassment. It was necessary to reassure colleagues that the design of the questionnaire pre-empted such possibilities.

Before discussing the results of the survey there is one other issue that needs to be addressed.

Is it possible to define a 'good' minister?

In 1998, the Methodist Conference adopted a report entitled 'The Review of the Role and Place of the Ordained Minister'.[15] The report drew on a large amount of information from around the Connexion, and noted in Section 2.2.1, a number of '. . . distinct polarities, or points at which the data received seemed to pull in opposite directions'. The report noted tensions between:

- the minister as set apart for service of the people; and the minister as called from within and remaining within the people with whom she or he serves;
- the minister as a commanding figure, able to manage, lead and unify; and the minister as companionable figure, who is friend, listener, team player;
- the expectation of omni-competence on the minister's behalf; and the supposition that the minister has limited gifts or abilities;
- the minister who represents or reconciles the whole; and the minister as having her or his own personal contribution to make;
- the minister as maintainer of the Church; and the minister as leader of evangelism and mission.

As previously stated, this tension is largely a product of the historical development of Methodism from a movement to an institution. In Wesley's day, frequent changes of minister (itinerancy) were supposed to protect preachers from becoming absorbed in pastoral care to the detriment of outreach and mission, and to defend the congregation against slipping into decline and heresy. However, as Methodist Societies have settled into stable congregations, the notion of preachers travelling to spread scriptural holiness throughout the land has lost some of its urgency. Furthermore, at present Methodism has insufficient presbyters to meet the demands of the circuits, at the same time as having more ministers per member than ever before. Consequently, there is considerable pressure on ministers (presbyters), collectively and individually, to meet the expectations of both congregations and the Church. The question is, expectations to do what?

Part of the purpose of the accompanied self-appraisal system was to find ways to help ministers elicit some of these expectations: to make overt the covert. As the current review of the scheme points out,[16] the system has developed differently in each district, and some aspects of the process have not worked as well in practice as was envisaged. Standing Orders require ministers to seek feedback on their ministry, which has largely been understood to mean written feedback. This has often restricted the individual minister to looking at 'doing' rather than 'being', and consequently the feedback has been limited and limiting.

One of the disadvantages of consulting on ministry is the suspicion with which such requests are treated.[17] For reasons already alluded to, some ministers feel very threatened by the suggestion that they are less than expert at the vast range of tasks that are demanded of them. This was made very evident by the anxious reaction of colleagues at the Superintendents' Meeting. As it turned out, the substantive questionnaire caused little concern, and the overall response was positive and encouraging. Anonymous, generalized comments about personal characteristics are relatively unthreatening, particularly when the characteristics offered are open to interpretation.

The questionnaire deliberately sought to use language that, in itself, was non-judgemental and disinterested. For example, the fact that some people might think that a 'good' minister is approachable purposefully avoids the question of what we might mean by 'approachable' in this context. What matters is not that there is a shared, objective understanding of approachability, but that some congregants, by their own definition, believe this is a positive attribute and the mark of a 'good' minister. Approachability may or may not be a virtue. It may indicate that the minister is over-familiar with congregants, or that she or he does not maintain appropriate boundaries, but this is not the point. The point is that, in a questionnaire that seeks to discover the attributes of a 'good' minister, some respondents value approachability.

It was for this reason that the study sought to consider what makes a minister 'good' – in the sense of quality and ability – rather than effective or competent. In order to make judgements about effectiveness or competency, there has to a standard against which effectiveness or competency can be measured, but the Methodist Church does not have such a standard. Ordained ministry is a vocation, not an occupation, ministers are not employees but office holders in the Church, and there is no job description. So Methodism, along with many mainstream denominations, is currently engaged in debates about how best to evaluate and appraise clergy.

In the current service for the Ordination of Presbyters, the President says to the newly ordained:

Remember your call.

Declare the Good News.
Celebrate the sacraments.
Serve the needy.
Minister to the sick.
Welcome the stranger.
Seek the lost.

Be shepherds to the flock of Christ.
As you exercise mercy, do not forget justice;
as you minister discipline, do not forget mercy;
that when Christ the Chief Shepherd comes in glory
he may count you among his faithful servants.[18]

Luscombe and Shreeve, in asking how presbyters are to be held accountable for the discharge of their call, eloquently describe the dilemma that faces the Methodist Church:

Is the accountability primarily to the whole Church, to local congregations, to the whole Methodist people as represented by Conference, or primarily to the college of presbyters of whom each individual is a part?[19]

Unfortunately, the evidence of ministerial colleagues suggests that the last people to whom presbyters would wish to be held accountable are local congregations.

One of the ways in which ministers and congregations avoid meaningful evaluation is through the notion that the qualities and attributes which contribute to the making of a 'good' minister are somehow mysterious and indefinable. They argue that 'good' ministers have a certain *je ne sais quoi* that defies definition or explanation. Any attempt to give an account of a 'good' minister quickly moves in to the minutiae of what we mean by the term 'good'. Since 'goodness' is conventionally so difficult to characterize in this context, the debate soon becomes sterile. Are there other notions that we can draw on to help us?

Virtue theory emphasizes the idea of a *good person* as someone who could be described also as an ethically admirable person. The classical account of the virtues is that of Aristotle,[20] who argues that virtues are dispositions of character, acquired by ethical training, displayed not just in action, but also in patterns of emotional reaction. Virtues are not just rigid habits, but are flexible under the application of practical reason. One advantage of current virtue theory is that it allows for interesting psychological connections between the ethical and other aspects of character, accepting that a person's temperament will have something to do with how a person conducts himself or herself ethically. Virtue theory is implicitly opposed to sharp boundaries between the moral and the non-moral. It is likely to acknowledge that there is a spectrum of desirable characteristics, and that no firm or helpful line can be drawn around those that are of especially moral significance. Furthermore, virtue theory recognizes the situational character of, in this case, ethical behaviour. All of us, as interpreters of ourselves and others, use shared concepts and models that have a history and a context. Any person's virtues depend, in many different ways, on his or her relation to society: they are constantly being shaped, interpreted and either reinforced or weakened. Applying this approach to the notion of the 'good' minister is helpful because, although we are not considering specifically a minister's *ethical* behaviour, the nature of the enquiry unavoidably implies it. Other studies, of completely different issues, have had to tackle the same question.

At the heart of the work of the Commission on Urban Life and Faith, for example, was the question: 'What makes a *good* city?' The Commission suggests that a good city is one that provides quality of life for its citizens and whose inhabitants have a sense of well-being. These are nebulous concepts, but research[21] suggests that, despite Britain's consistent economic growth and increasing standards of living, we do not necessarily feel any happier with our lives. In recent years, urban regeneration has become a multi-billion-pound industry, designed to renew our cities through economic investment. However, although prosperity is one of the factors that contributes to a city being identified as 'good', in the experience of some communities it is not automatically the most significant.

The Commission also argues that just because ideas such as happiness and well-being are imprecise, that does not mean they are valueless or without significance. On the contrary, a good city is a place where people find value and significance. For two years the Commission listened and consulted, and concluded that any regeneration strategy that did not start with the hopes and expectations of local people – that is, took seriously what local people value – was destined to fail. The *Faithful Cities* report suggests that a community's own understanding of its aspirations for its local environment is essential in the success of any regeneration strategy. It goes on to say:

> The Government's regeneration and renewal process involves clearly identifying your outcome and your target group, a process which might achieve accountability, but which, in the process, entraps us into reducing people to problems and issues.[22]

I am suggesting that any system of accountability for ministers that entails measuring effectiveness and competency (outcomes and performance indicators) without involving the values and perceptions of local congregations is likely to engender even more distrust and suspicion, similarly trapping us into reducing people (both congregants and ministers) to problems and issues. As the *Faithful Cities* report makes clear, asking the question matters, especially asking it in a way that generates opportunities for people to answer creatively.

However, implicit in asking the question are certain assumed values about what it means to be human, and what it means to be Christian. Similarly for this study, in asking what makes a 'good' minister 'good', I am assuming certain values about the nature of humanity, of human interaction, and the nature of community. I am also assuming that 'good' ministers exist, and that congregations have experience of them. Finally, I am assuming that it is possible to find a language that we can use to describe the characteristics and qualities of a 'good' minister, which, although it is rooted in the experience of the congregants, is sufficiently universal to be both meaningful and transferable.

Interestingly, the *Faithful Cities* report suggests that local churches have a role to play in regeneration by:

> . . . introducing the challenging and unfashionable idea of 'holiness' into the . . . process. This involves seeing people and their communities in all their complexity and in recognizing that they [we] don't always make rational sense. This is a long-term process which involves giving people full attention and entering a relationship with them.[23]

There seem to be some similarities here. Our communities are called to be holy (1 Peter 2.9), are complex, and we don't always make rational sense, but if Methodist congregations hold the key to meaningfully evaluating ministers, it will be a long-term process that will involve giving people full attention and entering a relationship with them. This is what Griffiths means when he says that Methodism needs to listen more carefully to its people, when it comes to giving an account of the minister.

So, what do the people say?

The questionnaire

There were 67 usable responses to the questionnaire. The profile of the respondents was as follows: 70% were female, 25% male, and 5% unknown; 63% were between 60 and 80 years of age, 19% between 40 and 60 years of age, and 15% over the age of 80; only 1.5% were under the age of 40. This corresponds to the demographic profile of the membership of the Methodist Church nationally.[24] All the respondents attended worship regularly, most describing themselves as attending virtually every week, and no one attended less frequently than every other week. Only 12 of the 67 respondents had not held office in the Church, and 89% described themselves as being committed and involved in the Methodist Church for a long time (over ten years).

Significantly, all respondents answered 'Yes' to the question, 'Have you ever had experience of someone you would describe as a "good" minister?'

The question that proved the most difficult for respondents to answer successfully was the one asking people to rank a minister's strengths from 1 to 8 (with 1 being high), against specifically identified areas of activity. Many of the responses *scored* the minister rather than *ranked* them. Nevertheless, 42 responses revealed that those respondents had distinct preferences for certain areas of ministerial activity.

Clearly, pastoral care is very much appreciated by certain members of congregations. For those to whom it is important, it is the *most* important. Teaching and evangelism, which are not initial priorities, demonstrate consistently high scoring in the middle rankings, which suggests that overall they are strengths valued by more people.

The additional areas of expertise supplied by respondents in the 'Other' category added to ideas offered in the questionnaire. Respondents made suggestions such as group planning, team work, ecumenical work,

Rank	Pastoral care	Teaching	Evangelism	Leadership	Admin.	Theology	Preaching
1	19	0	1	5	3	6	6
2	7	9	1	7	2	6	9
3	1	8	8	5	8	6	5
4	1	10	7	6	2	9	5
5	4	6	7	5	2	4	6
6	3	5	9	6	6	8	2
7	3	2	8	4	15	2	5
8	3	0	1	2	3	1	8

Figure 1. Ranking the strengths of a 'good' minister.

interfaith relations, and experience outside of the ministry. Others ranked personal qualities such as enthusiasm, a good sense of humour, friendship, willingness to listen, kindness and fun, approachability, and availability. Respondents who scored rather than ranked the listed abilities also added comments such as, 'I cannot choose', or 'A good all-rounder', indicating that the 'good' minister is multi-talented. It certainly seems to be the case that, apart from a particular emphasis on pastoral care, respondents characteristically expect a 'good' minister to have a range of skills and be passably competent in a number of areas.

One question asked respondents to consider the effect that the 'good' minister had upon them. The categories were designed specifically to elicit both internal and external responses. For example, 'Be aware of God's presence' is an internal response, one that relies purely on the felt response of the individual. However, 'Increase my giving' is an external response, one that has a concrete, demonstrable effect, with measurable direct consequences. External categories scored considerably less frequently than internal ones. Respondents seemed to experience the effect of a 'good' minister on their lives more in terms of inner, felt reactions, rather than outer, demonstrable consequences (see Figure 2).

Of course, classifying the categories in this way is inexact and open to question. It could be argued that 'Acknowledge my sinfulness', for example, is an external process, requiring a degree of objectivity on the part of the respondent. Nevertheless, for the purposes of the survey it was important to begin to separate out the ways in which a 'good' minister might have an impact on a person's private sense of self and their relationship with God, from the ways in which a 'good' minister might have an impact on a person's public sense of self and their relationship with others. Certainly, the least favoured categories were also the most personally exposing; particularly in a questionnaire that was inviting people to participate in follow-up interviews.

Question 11 was designed to force respondents into making judgements about the most important characteristics of a 'good' minister. Respondents could choose only five qualities, one of which could be of their own making. Nine respondents did not complete the question satisfactorily. Approachability, ability to listen to people, a sense of vision, an ability to help people discover a vision, and confidentiality were undoubtedly the characteristics most valued by respondents. 'Good' ministers are certainly not expected to do what the congregation wants, be in charge, tell people what to do, or know what is right. Neither are they necessarily required to know what to do, avoid conflict, know what they want, or keep people in order.

Seven respondents gave additional suggestions in the 'Other' category. There was an emphasis on team work and collaboration, and preaching. More than one respondent mentioned humour.

Having required people to make judgements about some of the characteristics of a 'good' minister, the purpose of Question 12 was to ascertain respondents' strength of feeling about those characteristics.

Because of the variables involved, these results are quite complex and require interpretation that is more sophisticated. For example, at first glance it appears that respondents overwhelmingly believe that a 'good' minister keeps confidentiality, with 69% strongly holding this view. However, 95% of respondents believe that a 'good' minister respects difference, and half (47.5%) strongly agree with the statement. Similarly, 48% believe that a 'good' minister should try to please the people, but 43% disagree with this view, so here opinions are more evenly balanced, although 12% of those who disagree with the statement do so strongly. When it comes to the minister being morally superior to the people, 71% do not concur with the statement, 49% disagree and 22% strongly disagree. A 'good' minister, however, is not expected to agree with everyone; 85% disagreed with the statement, 28% of them strongly. Interestingly, whether or not a 'good' minister should keep out of trouble with the congregation was slightly more contentious: 22% thought he or she should, but 60% did not. Unlike the responses to the previous question, there were distinct preferences for the minister to keep control (60% agreed, 15% strongly agreed); and offer strong leadership (48% agreed, 46% strongly agreed).

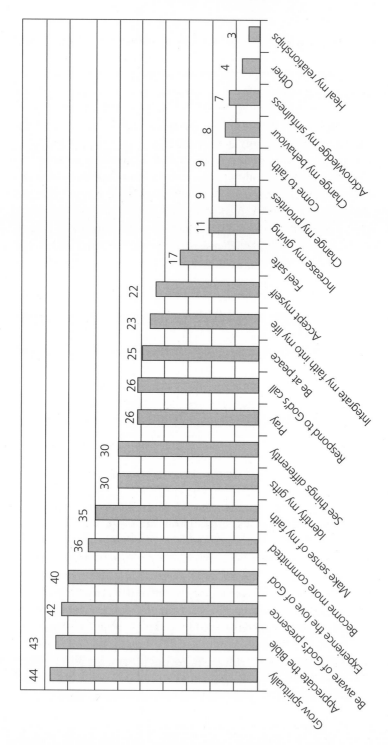

Figure 2. Collated results to Question 10.

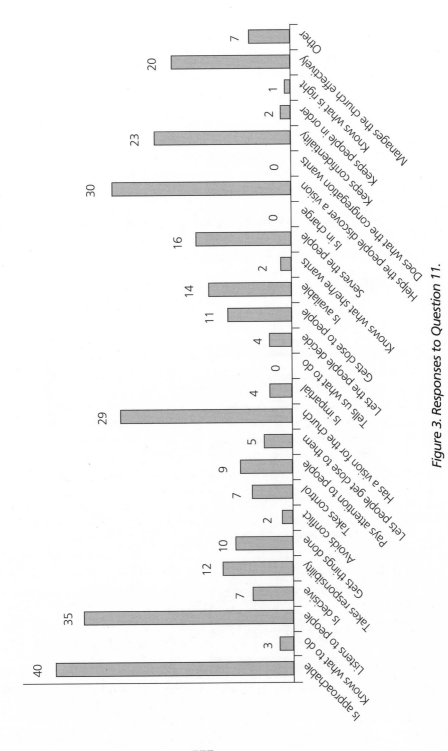

Figure 3. Responses to Question 11.

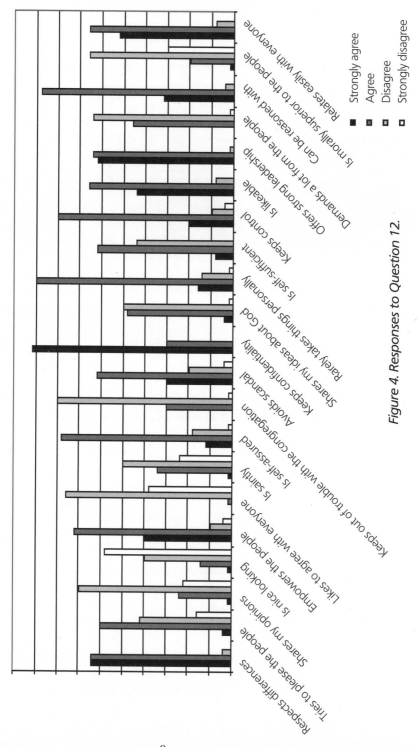

Figure 4. Responses to Question 12.

Strongly agree
Agree
Disagree
Strongly disagree

Relates easily with everyone
Is morally superior to the people
Can be reasoned with
Demands a lot from the people
Offers strong leadership
Is likeable
Keeps control
Is self-sufficient
Rarely takes things personally
Shares my ideas about God
Keeps confidentiality
Avoids scandal
Is self-assured
Keeps out of trouble with the congregation
Is saintly
Likes to agree with everyone
Empowers the people
Is nice looking
Shares my opinions
Tries to please the people
Respects differences

Some of the categories in this question considered the minister's personal attributes. Respondents indicated that a 'good' minister is someone who is self-assured (58% agreed, 9% strongly agreed), rarely take things personally (67% agreed, 12% strongly agreed), is self-sufficient (46% agreed, 6% strongly agreed), and relates easily to people (66% agreed, 24% strongly agreed). Most respondents would expect to find a good minister likeable (49% agreed, 33% strongly agreed); happily, they do not expect him or her to be necessarily nice looking (33% disagreed, 43% strongly disagreed).

One category asked the extent to which respondents agreed that a 'good' minister was saintly. Interestingly, 25% agreed that he or she would be, whereas 37% disagreed and 18% strongly disagreed with the statement. When it came to Question 13, belief about the holiness of a 'good' minister, only two respondents did not complete this question. Of the remaining 65 responses, 15 said 'Yes' and 50 (75%) said 'No'. In planning the questionnaire, one of the suppositions had been that congregants would expect 'good' ministers somehow to exemplify characteristics that were more virtuous and morally superior to those of the ordinary people, hence the inclusion of the categories regarding moral superiority and saintliness, and specifically this question. Clearly, three-quarters of respondents did not expect a greater degree of godliness from a 'good' minister than they did from ordinary members of the congregation.

The final question asked what the respondent believed was the essential quality that made a 'good' minister good. Fifty-five respondents (82%) chose to make a free text contribution and offer suggestions about what they saw these essential qualities to be. These ranged from one-word answers ('approachability'), to several sentences, listing various qualities. To analyse these contributions, key words in the texts were identified, and then grouped into categories: vocational attributes, personal qualities, people skills, management skills, focus, and other. Of course, this approach to analysing text is not exact and is open to bias; it relies heavily on the analyst interpreting the intended meaning of the respondent. However, given the request for 'essential' qualities, and limited space for responses, some consistency was possible.

Once again, respondents identified pastoral care and concern as the key characteristic of a 'good' minister. A 'good' minister is also inclusive and concerned for all ages. He or she listens and communicates well, can preach, has a visible faith and is close to God. A 'good' minister offers leadership, guidance and direction, both spiritually and practically. She or he is not remote but gets close to people. A 'good' minister is essentially human.

Vocational attributes		People skills	
Close to God	6	Accessible language	3
Love of God	4	Communication	9
Christ centred	2	Listens	7
Brings others to faith	1	Approachability	3
Visible faith	7	Availability	2
Vision for church	3	Adaptability	2
Preaching	7	Interpersonal skills	3
Prayer	2		
Bible knowledge/exposition	1	**Management skills**	
Pastoral care and concern	15	Knows the church organization	1
Commitment	2	Organized	2
		Team player	1
Personal qualities		Confidentiality	1
Integrity	3	Leadership	7
Self-aware	2	Spiritual journey/guidance/direction	5
Encouraging	2	Manage change (modern methods)	1
Humour	3		
Human/not 'holier than thou'	4	**Focus**	
Gets close to people	4	World's issues	3
Sensitivity	1	Community	5
A friend	1	Family focus	1
Enjoyment of role	1	All ages (inclusive)	11
Sincerity	2		
Compassion	2	**Other**	
		Not necessary to be ordained	1
		Commands respect	1
		Faith and actions congruent	2
		Experience of life	2

Figure 5. The essential qualities of a 'good' minister.

What does it all mean?

Clearly, as far as the respondents are concerned, the important characteristics of a 'good' minister are the gifts of pastoral care, preaching and leadership, combined with a vision for the church. Their important personal qualities are those of approachability, the ability to listen, the ability to relate to all kinds of people, and the ability to help people discover a vision for themselves. A 'good' minister offers strong leadership, keeps control, and empowers the people. He or she is self-assured, rarely takes things personally, and can be reasoned with. A 'good' minister is likeable, relates easily with everyone and respects differences. If possible, he or she avoids scandal. A 'good' minister absolutely observes confidentiality.

None of this is particularly surprising, even if some of it appears to be a little self-contradictory. However, the survey results do raise a number of interesting points. First, 'good' ministers are not perfect. Contrary to some expectations,[25] the overall view of congregants is realistic. In fact, one of the identified characteristics of a 'good' minister was that he or she is aware of their strengths and weaknesses and allows others with complementary gifts to support them. Furthermore, congregants have a balanced view of how a 'good' minister might interact with a congregation. 'Good' ministers are not acquiescent or compliant. They are not expected to share congregants' opinions. On the contrary, there is an expectation that some conflict is inevitable, perhaps even healthy.

The strong support for the idea that a 'good' minister is self-assured, and rarely takes things personally, was particularly interesting. As stated earlier, there were assumptions in the design of the questionnaire that 'good' ministers are seen to demonstrate healthy personality characteristics, like autonomy, flexibility and attachment. Stewart and Joines[26] describe autonomy as the psychological state of being connected to three capacities: awareness, spontaneity and intimacy. Autonomy involves behaving, thinking and feeling in response to the here-and-now reality, rather than past experiences. One possible explanation for the respondents' suggestion that 'good' ministers are self-assured and do not take things personally, may be an appreciation of ministers who can act autonomously, and are able to keep their egos out of situations and relationships. As leaders and public figures in communities, ministers are objects for both admiration and vilification, neither of which may have anything to do with the minister personally. Sometimes people can be very angry with God, and the minister is the nearest person to God to which they have access, so the minister becomes the focus for the anger.

Similarly, because the minister can be seen as a parental figure, some people may project onto the minister all manner of feelings about their parents or other significant people from their past. This is especially likely for people who have a poor sense of their own boundaries, or for those experiencing a crisis, for example bereavement. It is extremely important that ministers are aware of these possibilities and do not collude with this phenomenon that psychologists refer to as transference. This can be particularly difficult when the projected feelings are those of approval and admiration.

It is also possible that the notions of strong leadership, keeping control and avoiding scandal are linked to this ability. Respondents may be indicating that one of the qualities of a 'good' minister is the ability to establish and maintain clear psychological boundaries, while relating easily with everyone. Clearly, respondents want ministers to be likeable, but one of the potential criticisms of ministers who seek to be 'likeable' is that they fail to keep professional distance; that is, they inappropriately blur the boundaries between their relationships. However, there is a fine distinction between professional distance and detachment or remoteness, which respondents appear to appreciate.

Furthermore, the positive ability to relate easily to people does seem to be something that respondents identify as the quality of a 'good' minister. Perhaps, when balanced against the other identified gifts of leadership, control and self-assurance, this is not so much a contradiction as respondents affirming that, above all else, they want the minister to be the minister. Likeability and empowerment are all very well, but not at the expense of losing the ministerial identity of the person who has been ordained to embody that role.

A common thread?

What is it possible to claim, based on these findings? It appears that the Methodist people do know what makes a minister, and they have an idea about what makes a 'good' minister. The common thread in the evidence suggests that one of the characteristics of 'good' ministers is that they are able to make appropriate, meaningful relationships with a wide range of people, and that they are seen to be doing it. At first glance, this may seem unremarkable, but it is the public nature of this attribute that is particularly noteworthy. Ministers are believed to be 'good' because congregants observe them behaving in ways that congregants perceive to be consonant with the making of appropriate, meaningful relationships. In short, 'good' ministers are perceived to make what is known in psychological terms as 'good' attachments.

In order to make the significant point about 'good' ministers and 'good' attachments, it will be helpful to give a very brief overview of this theory, which was developed by John Bowlby[27] in the post-war period, and gives an account of the effects of emotional attachment and separation in infancy on subsequent psychological development. The theory grew out of studying children separated from their families following the evacuation at the start of the Second World War, and attempts to explain the lived experience of 'When I am close to my loved one I feel good, when I am far away I feel anxious, sad and lonely.'

To feel attached is to feel safe and secure. Babies and infants have a predisposition to make attachments to significant adults (usually parents), for obvious reasons of dependency. However, for an attachment to be effective it needs to be mutual. Babies *attach* to parents, parents *bond* with babies. To establish this reciprocity, parental figures need to respond to attachment behaviour (looking, hearing and holding) from the child and engage in active, reciprocal interaction. The purpose of attachment is to establish a secure base[28] from which the child can feel sufficiently confident to begin to explore the world. Secure attachments eventually enable the child to create an internal working model of himself or herself and others, based on repeated patterns of interactive experience. A securely attached child will store an internal working model of a responsive, loving, reliable caregiver, and of a self that is worthy of love and attention, and will bring these assumptions to bear on all other relationships. Conversely, an insecurely attached child may view the world as a dangerous place in which other people are to be treated with great caution, and see himself or herself as ineffective and unworthy of love. These internal models continue into adult life.

In the follow-up interviews, the behaviours described and the language used by the interviewees further indicated that a 'good' minister demonstrates secure attachment behaviour, and publicly models active, reciprocal interaction with congregants. This encourages them to associate the minister with a felt experience of a secure base. It is possible to argue that when this happens, ministers are experienced as warm and approachable, emotionally reliable and trustworthy. The crucial aspect of this behaviour is that it is genuine, consistent and public. Genuine, in that the minister is securely attached (internally) to themselves, to others and to God: consistent, in that the minister's beliefs about themselves, about others and about God are congruent with their behaviour: and public, in that ministers are manifestly seen to embody and self-consciously live out these characteristics in the community. This is the minister 'modelling the Christian life' mentioned earlier.

In 1974, the Methodist Conference adopted a statement on 'Ordination',[29] which extends the Deed of Union as follows:

> As a perpetual reminder of this calling and as a means of being obedient to it, the Church sets aside men and women, specially called, in ordination. In their office the calling of the whole Church is focused and represented, and it is their responsibility as representative persons to lead the people to share with them in that calling. In this sense they are the sign of the presence and ministry of Christ in the Church, and through the Church to the world.

Howcroft[30] suggests that the language of 'signs', used in the 1974 statement, is important, and uses the notions of prophetic signs and iconic signs to illustrate his view. He notes that for signs to be effective there has to be an agreement that they point to something, and states, 'Signs are functions in negotiated systems of meaning.' He then proposes that in relation to ministers, theologically, God may be seen as an active party in the negotiation. Thus, as a result of negotiation among human beings and between human beings and God, those ordained are empowered to be iconic signs that act as mirrors of Christ and the Church.

I would like to suggest that, by applying attachment theory, this works psychologically too. If God is an active party in the negotiated system of meaning about what makes a minister, then it may be possible to argue that one of the other characteristics of a 'good' minister is that they enable congregants to attach to God. This might go some way towards explaining the emphasis on the internal experiences demonstrated in Figure 2. It also helps to give an account of the apparent contradictions in the responses to Question 11.

Congregants seem to understand and appreciate that 'good' ministers preserve proper relationships and act in ways that are impartial and non-exploitative. The suggestion of a secure attachment metaphor is not an excuse for poor boundary maintenance. On the contrary, the ability to make quality attachments is much more likely to support ministerial identity and help maintain clear boundaries. The concept of professional distance is important in other helping professions, but ministers are not doctors with patients, or social workers with clients; they are participant leaders in communities. However, because of the leadership role, relationships between ministers and congregants always involve power. So, ministers need to be aware of the ways in which certain relationships and behaviours, or other people's perceptions of those relationships and behaviours, can affect their ability to carry out their role. The capacity to make good attachments enables ministers to act professionally, while engaging in profound and significant relationships which are highly valued by the people.

Conclusion

This study was a small-scale, low-key piece of research, to find out if people in our churches knew what makes a minister, and, more specifically, what makes a 'good' minister. As a result, although it is not possible to say definitively that there is a general view among congregants about what constitutes a 'good' minister, there are clearly some identifiable qualities that are highly valued. Of the vocational gifts, pastoral care, preaching and leadership are the most significant. Of the personal qualities, approachability, the ability to keep confidentiality and a sense of vision are the most appreciated. These responses to the questionnaires and the interviews lead me to believe that it is possible to establish a definition of 'good' ministry and of a 'good' minister, and that attachment theory may make a contribution in helping us critically analyse how that works. In some senses, categorizing gifts in this way is arbitrary, and one unifying characteristic could be that a 'good' minister demonstrates attachment behaviour, which offers congregants a secure base from which to explore their faith and move out into the world in mission.

The study also revealed how infrequently members of Methodist churches are asked their opinion about such matters. Although the Accompanied Self-Appraisal scheme theoretically canvassed the views of congregants, this was localized, personalized and fraught with difficulty. It is encouraging to discover, therefore, that the people in Methodist churches do recognize good ministry when they encounter it and are able to articulate some of the characteristics that make a 'good' minister good. Moreover, they do appreciate much of the ministry that they receive. There does seem to be an understanding that ministers are human beings who struggle, along with all Christians, to live with integrity the life of the baptized. This is profoundly encouraging for any future work that enables congregants to participate more constructively in the ongoing development of ministers.

The questionnaire

CONFIDENTIAL

Facts about you (Please circle as appropriate, or highlight if you are doing this electronically.)

1 Are you: Male   Female

2 Aged: 12 yrs or under   13–19   20–29   30–39   40–59   60–79   80+

3 How would you describe yourself?

Black or Black British-Caribbean	Black or Black British-African
Other Black background	Asian or Asian British
Chinese	Korean
Other Asian background	White British
White other	Mixed – White and Afro-Caribbean
Mixed – White and Asian	Other Mixed background
Other Ethnic background	

4 For how long have you been associated with the church?

Under 1 year   1–2 years   3–5 years   5–10 years   Over 10 years

5 How would you describe your worship attendance? (Circle one.)

Virtually every week   3 weeks out of 4   Every other week   Once a month

Once every 6 weeks   Once every 3 months   Occasionally   Major festivals only

6 On a scale 1–5, how would you describe your participation in the life of the church?

non-participatory   generally very active

1   2   3   4   5

7 Do you hold, or have you ever held, an office in the church (e.g. steward, local preacher, church council representative)?

Yes   No

From your experience

8 Have you ever had experience of someone you would describe as a 'good' minister?

Yes   No

9 How would you rank this minister's particular strengths? (Please rank from 1–8, with 1 as the highest and 8 the lowest. Do not use any number more than once.)

Pastoral care   [   ]
Teaching   [   ]
Evangelism   [   ]
Leadership   [   ]
Administration   [   ]
Theology (what they believed about God)   [   ]
Preaching   [   ]
Other (please state)   [   ]

10 What was the effect of this 'good' minister on you? (Please tick any which apply.)

Helped me to…

Grow spiritually	
Appreciate the Bible	
Be aware of God's presence	
Experience the love of God	
Become more committed	
Make sense of my faith	
Identify my gifts	
See things differently	
Pray	
Respond to God's call	
Be at peace	
Integrate my faith into my life	
Accept myself	
Feel safe	
Increase my giving	
Change my priorities	
Come to faith	
Change my behaviour	
Acknowledge my sinfulness	
Heal my relationships	
Other (please state below)	

Other...

In your opinion

11 Which of the following would you consider the most important characteristics of a 'good' minister? (Tick 5.)

Is approachable		Lets the people decide	
Knows what to do		Gets close to people	
Listens to people		Is available	
Is decisive		Knows what she/he wants	
Takes responsibility		Serves the people	
Gets things done		Is in charge	
Avoids conflict		Helps the people discover a vision	
Takes control		Does what the congregation wants	
Pays attention to people		Keeps confidentiality	
Lets people get close to them		Keeps people in order	
Has a vision for the church		Knows what is right	
Is impartial		Manages the church effectively	
Tells us what to do		Other (please state below)	

Other..

12 To what extent do you agree with the following statements? (Please tick as appropriate.)

A good minister…	Strongly agree	Agree	Disagree	Strongly disagree
Respects differences				
Tries to please the people				
Shares my opinions				
Is nice looking				
Empowers the people				
Likes to agree with everyone				
Is saintly				
Is self-assured				
Keeps out of trouble with the congregation				

A good minister…	Strongly agree	Agree	Disagree	Strongly disagree
Avoids scandal				
Keeps confidentiality				
Shares my ideas about God				
Rarely takes things personally				
Is self-sufficient				
Keeps control				
Is likeable				
Offers strong leadership				
Demands a lot from the people				
Can be reasoned with				
Is morally superior to the people				
Relates easily with everyone				

13 Do you believe that ministers should be holier than members of the congregation? (Please circle/highlight.)

Yes   No

14. What, in your opinion, is the essential quality that makes a 'good' minister 'good'?

....

....

....

....

....

....

Would you be willing to participate in a follow-up interview? (Please circle/highlight.)

Yes   No

If *yes*, please write your name, address and telephone number below.

Thank you for completing this survey.

Notes

1 For an overview of congregational studies in the UK, see for example M. Guest, K. Tustin and L. Woodhead, *Congregational Studies in the UK*, London: Ashgate, 2004.

2 J. F. Hopewell, *Congregation: Stories and Structures*, London: SCM Press, 1987.

3 N. T. Ammerman, J. W. Carroll, C. S. Dudley and W. McKinney, *Studying Congregations: A New Handbook*, Nashville: Abingdon, 1998.

4 J. M. Haley and L. J. Francis, *British Methodism: What Circuit Ministers Really Think*, Peterborough: Epworth Press, 2006.

5 Deed of Union, clause 4. The current form of the Deed of Union is to be found in Volume 2 of *The Constitutional Practice and Discipline of the Methodist Church*, Peterborough: Methodist Publishing House, published annually.

6 *The Ministry of the People of God*, a report to the 1988 Methodist Conference, in *Statements and Reports of the Methodist Church on Faith and Order, Volume 2, 1984–2000, Part One*, Peterborough: Methodist Publishing House, 2000.

7 In 1995, the Methodist Conference reaffirmed the judgement of the 1993 Conference that the Methodist Church had recognized and received the diaconate from God as an order of ministry. Consequently, the term 'presbyter' came into use in Methodism to distinguish a particular category of ordained person from that of 'deacon'.

8 Leslie Griffiths, 'What is a Presbyter?', in *What is a Minister?*, P. Luscombe and E. Shreeve (eds), Peterborough: Epworth Press, 2002.

9 Griffiths, 'What is a Presbyter?', p. 18.

10 I am using the word 'good' here in terms of quality and ability, rather than in its moral or behavioural sense.

11 Of course, it may be possible that age, gender and marital status are factors in determining a 'good' minister, but the study was not designed to consider this.

12 F. N. Kerlinger, *Foundations of Behavioural Research*, Austin: Holt, Rinehart and Winston, 1970.

13 Eric Berne, *Transactional Analysis in Psychotherapy*, London: Souvenir Press, 2001.

14 See, for example, Berne (2001, 2004), Harries (1995), and Stewart and Joines (1987). Also Bowlby (1997, 2004).

15 Methodist Church, 'The Review of the Role and Place of the Ordained Minister', in Conference Agenda 1998, Peterborough: Methodist Publishing House, 1998.

16 *ASA Ten Years On*, report to the Methodist Conference 2006

17 Interestingly, the ASA review pointed out that requests for feedback about the scheme itself have met with little success.

18 *Methodist Worship Book*, Peterborough: Methodist Publishing House, 1999, p. 308.

19 Luscombe and Shreeve, *What is a Minister?*, p. 163.

20 See Aristotle, *Nicomachean Ethics*, New York: Dover Publications, 1998. Also D. Bostock, *Aristotle's Ethics*, Oxford: Oxford University Press, 2000.

21 See, for example, the Roman Catholic report, *The Common Good* (English

and Welsh Bishops, 1996), the Salvation Army report, *The Paradox of Prosperity* (1999), and the ecumenical reports, *Unemployment and the Future of Work* (CTBI, 1997) and *Prosperity with a Purpose: Christians and the Ethics of Affluence* (CTBI, 2005).

22 *Faithful Cities, the Report from the Commission on Urban Life and Faith*, jointly published by MPH and Church House Publishing, 2006, p. 58.

23 *Faithful Cities*, p. 59.

24 See Philip Escott and Alison Gelder, *Church Life Profile 2001: Denominational Results for the Methodist Church*, London: Churches Information for Mission. 2002.

25 One of the concerns of the Superintendents' Meeting was that such enquiry would merely expose the impossible expectations of church members.

26 I. Stewart and V. Joines, *Transactional Analysis Today*, North Carolina: Lifespace Publishing, 1987.

27 John Bowlby, *Attachment and Loss: Vol. 1: Attachment*, London: Pimlico Press, 1997. John Bowlby, *Attachment and Loss: Vol. 2: Separation: Anxiety and Anger*, London: Pimlico Press, 2004, originally published in 1969 and 1973.

28 Mary Ainsworth first used the term 'a secure base' to describe the ambience created by the attachment figure for the attached person. See Mary Ainsworth, *Attachment: Retrospect and Prospect*, in C. M. Parkes and J. Stevenson-Hinde (eds), *The Place of Attachment in Human Behaviour*, Bedford: Tavistock, 1982.

29 In *Statements of the Methodist Church on Faith and Order 1933–1983*, rev. edn, 2000, pp. 108–19.

30 K. Howcroft, 'Ministerial Roles in Methodism' in Luscombe and Shreeve, *What is a Minister?*, p. 139.